Tony -
You have been such a
great friend to me for almost
30 years !!! We have had a
"clearly fun" life !
Love,
Dawn
6-13-09

WOMAN-OWNED BUSINESS

by

Dawn Dallaire
with Linda Lee Ratto, Ed.M.

First Published 2008
Penman Publishers

WOMAN-OWNED BUSINESS

by Dawn Dallaire
with Linda Lee Ratto, Ed.M.

ISBN: 978-1-932496-64-2

Front cover photograph by Ellen Whiten, "Scoop Magazine"
Back Cover "New Dawn" photograph by Ian Robert Mari

Edited by:
Karen Brown
Ray Hammond

Manufactured in the United States of America.

DEDICATION

To Larry Brown, the greatest businessman I know. Thank you for being my mentor, my confidant, my supporter, but most of all my friend.

ACKNOWLEDGEMENTS

I would like to thank everyone who has helped me through my journey. First of all, to my family, thank you for your continuous support. I know it's been especially hard on all of you. To my parents for raising me and believing in me each and every day. To all my good friends, thank you all for being there for me. To my many business associates, thank you for all your help. And finally, a special thanks to everyone who has ever come into my life. You have all played a part and I am eternally grateful.

PREFACE

My goal for this book is to share my story in hopes of helping you continue your own story. Why do I use the words "continue your own story"? The fact that you're reading this book tells me that you've already begun your story and a fresh chapter in your life. Perhaps you are well along on your business venture. Perhaps you're just starting. No matter which – continue, continue, continue creating and persevere. As you go along, please read my story knowing you are not alone. Please know that my trials and triumphs will help you.

My biggest complaint in building my business is that "business-making" doesn't come with an owner's manual. While I certainly don't profess to be an expert, here I have documented the challenges and solutions I learned over the years. I trust my story will inspire you, make you laugh, and most of all bring something into your life to learn and apply to your own story. I continue to evolve my life story and my business story and I would love to hear from you if this book helps you succeed in refreshing and renewing your life.

I am fortunate that I had a business mentor early on. From the very first email I realized that what this man was telling me was valuable. He was generous and gracious to share his wealth of business knowledge with me. It's the business principles and lessons that he and others have given me that inspired this book. The emails have served as a journal for the trials and triumphs of *Clearly Fun Soap (CFS)*.

TABLE OF CONTENTS

Chapter 1 --- 1
    MY BUSINESS STORY

Chapter 2 -- 11
    PASSION, PERSISTENCE...

Chapter 3 -- 17
    GETTING STARTED...and also being a Mother

Chapter 4 -- 25
    IMPORTING, EXPORTING and DOMESTIC SHIPPING

Chapter 5 -- 33
    PUBLIC RELATIONS

Chapter 6 -- 40
    THE "OTHER" CHALLENGE...My Health and Weight Loss

Chapter 7 -- 50
    MARKETING and PACKAGING

Chapter 8 -- 55
    BUSINESS BASICS

PICTURE PAGES -- 60

Chapter 9 -- 66
    WHEN TO GROW, HOW TO GROW

Chapter 10 --- 78
    PLAYING WITH THE "BIG BOYS"

Chapter 11 --- 83
    TRADESHOWS

Chapter 12 --- 90
    FINANCING YOUR BUSINESS

Chapter 13 --- 98
    EGGS IN ONE BASKET

Chapter 14 -- 101
    BALANCING PERSONAL and PROFESSIONAL LIFE

Chapter 15 -- 105
    BENEFITS OF BEING A WOMAN IN BUSINESS

Chapter 16 -- 110
    INTERVIEWS WITH ENTREPRENEURS

Appendix -- 115

Mentor Moments

~ Business is fun! It is not always easy, but it sure is fun.

~ Don't give your power away. Is one business service better than another? Are the big names better than you? No.

~ Credit report services or listings in Dun and Bradstreet have their reputations. These services do collect information free and then charge others for it. Think. Assess for yourself. Ask your teammates and trusted friends. You can neither guarantee, nor buy success. Obtain information about companies you wish to market and sell to, but stop at sending your financials around. When you need credit, yes, selectively place your valuable information to only your clients or potential lenders.

~ In preparation for obtaining a building or expanding, establish sales records to show your lenders and remember this: always, always pay your bills on time.

~ We are all 'once in a lifetime' people if we'll do what we are supposed to... (that is, be in your life-purpose!)

INTRODUCTION
COMMITMENT

Commitment means to follow through to the end. It is a word you cannot take lightly.

"The End" can mean until the final project is completed or it can mean to the end of your life. In either case, make sure you love what you are doing so you can commit to finishing your venture. Commitment has to be strong and steadfast so on those occasions when you feel like giving up, you can lean on your conviction, on the fact that this is a life purpose for you.

A cheap commitment is like a cheap apology. It doesn't hold up. Be a woman of your word and commit through and through to the end. For example, the writing of this book has tested my commitment to follow through. It hasn't come easy, yet I've loved every minute of it. It is a loving commitment I have made to myself, with others and God. Therefore, I hand you my commitment, *Woman Owned Business*, with the intention that sharing my story will assist you in your commitment in whatever business brings you joy and satisfaction.

> ### Path-Crosser
> Anyone who crosses your path whom you allow to have an influence in your life. By this I mean that I am always open to learning from those I meet.   ~D. Dallaire

Chapter 1
MY BUSINESS STORY

As I look back on my business story, I realize that it actually began when I was a little girl. My grandfather started E.D. Green & Sons, after retiring from Texaco. My father was in high school when his dad started the business and my dad worked there until I was in first grade. He left the family business and started his own, Pioneer Fluid Power Company, which he ran until he sold it on his sixtieth birthday. So all of my life I was a part of privately owned family businesses.

When I was very young, my brother, sister and I would go to my dad's business on the weekends. We hooked paperclips together and drove the secretaries crazy. On Mondays the secretaries would reach for a paper clip and grab a whole string of them. We found great pleasure in this! Later on I worked part-time for my dad throughout high school and over the summers and whenever I was home from college.

Thinking back, I was never really interested in the business and thought I hadn't paid much attention. After all, it was an air compressor business and that field didn't hold much interest for a young girl. I realized years later, in 2003, when I launched Clearly Fun Soap, that I had paid close attention. While I sell soap and Daddy sold air compressors, the business structure and my own business philosophy are much the same. I apply many of the work ethic principles that my father did. I enjoy relying on his guidance to this day.

In 1982 I married my husband, John Dallaire, from Maine. His family owned an amusement park there. As soon as the honeymoon was over, we headed to the beautiful state of Maine, a brand new beginning in a new territory for me. We arrived in early March to an abundance of snow. I'm from the south and it was freezing! There were "potholes" everywhere! Having come from the south, I'd never experienced so many potholes. That would prove only the tip of my iceberg, as they say. It was transition time—big-time.

I went from a full-time college student, with a part-time job, having a boyfriend (John), playing basketball and running three miles a day to no physical exercise. It was too cold! Plus, as a new wife, my role was making lunch and dinner every day for John and me. (I don't do breakfast, even now.) Married life and my new location was surely foreign territory to me. It wasn't long before I started packing on the pounds. Because of my athletic and very busy student life, I'd never even worried about my weight. Looking back now, I think my lifestyle change was drastic. I stayed inside a lot and thought the snow would never go away when we had a late April snow blizzard of several feet.

Of course, the snow did melt, although not for too many months. It seemed to me that June was far too late for nice weather. By then I was gaining weight fast. At last, I was to do something else other than cook and eat. John's mother owned an ice cream shop, which she asked me to run. I was grateful for the challenge, yet had no clue what to do and little training. At just barely twenty years old, I was not equipped to handle the stress of my new French family and this summer business. Back home in summer our family swam and took it easier than during the rest of the business year. Not so for the new family of very hard-working and enterprising entrepreneurs.

The intense summer tourist hours were long and hard and I was miserable trying to adjust that first summer. His mother, owner of the business, was well-meaning, but critical of the job I was doing. Her strong personality was too much for me because every time she walked by this Sweet Shoppe, she had some criticism, something to correct. I know now that she was trying to train me and help, but I was exhausted, not thinking straight and trying to please my new family. It seemed I could do nothing right. It felt difficult to tell my employees what to do because it felt as if I was hurting their feelings. So, I let them run all over me, taking advantage. It was challenging, as most of them were summer workers, my age or even older, and didn't want me—the owner's daughter-in-law—telling them what to do. I made up for this by working hard, doing their jobs and mine. I cried myself to sleep many nights. Top that with my new eating ice cream habit and my weight soared. To relax and get a break, I went driving. I'd grab some fast food and eat and ride. I couldn't seem to find myself and the weight gain added to my desperation. I loved my husband very much, yet I had no idea at that tender age what was happening to me. It was work and eat, work and eat. And I in no way blame anyone but myself.

One of the things I learned, especially with these years of weight struggle experiences behind me, is that each of us is ultimately responsible for our health. It isn't just "weight gain" for me, it is my health. That's how I look at my history and my life now. I am my own "Pilot in Command." I wish I'd known this from the beginning of my weight gain, but I know it now. I wish it hadn't taken me so many years—over two decades—to realize this personal responsibility and do something about it. I know now that I will make whatever changes I need to in order to keep control of my health, no matter what it costs. We all are in charge of ourselves. You and I cannot do the things we wish to do, make our dreams for our businesses come true, if we don't have our health.

In 1997 the family sold the amusement park and we headed back down south, having two children, and being a dedicated at-home mom. In 2000, my husband, John, came home and told me he was no longer going to build houses. For years as a small business owner and contractor, John encountered some nasty homeowners and just plain refused to build another home. Panic slowly swelled within me, as we had no savings and little extra money between house profits on which to fall back. It didn't take long before we began to sink. I didn't know what to do or where to turn. I weighed almost 300 pounds and felt that I was completely unemployable, a "non-hire". I could not stand on my feet for long, was always tired and felt virtually disabled. John began driving a school bus part time so we could have health insurance. The insurance was great but the pay could not cover our house mortgage, nor support our family of four. So John and my dad began clearing out land and developing a neighborhood to sell the lots to other builders. This was encouraging, but took several years to complete. The credit card debt mounted and all of this stress made my weight soar even more.

Business brings out the best and perhaps the worst in people...I am the kind of person who is so deeply non-confrontational that I would rather weigh 300 pounds than say something that would hurt someone's feelings. Here lay my life challenges. To date, I work with a counselor on this and I journal and reflect on my life periodically because it is good for me.

I can safely say that my business has helped me grow personally, as well as street-wise/business-wise. I realize—actually I now know *deep* within myself—that most of the time when I state my truth or express my opinion that it is *not* confrontational, it is simply my opinion. I also realize that my opinion as CEO of a corporation matters. Honestly, I am managing my business (and my life) better every day. My new life habit of self reflection—sparked by writing this book and clarifying my life through writing—continuously assists me in improving myself. No personal trait is insurmountable when you focus on learning a different attitude and outlook. I know I have looked at myself in the mirror and the reflection is definitely improving and blossoming!

Back to my recent past: What could I do? What could I contribute as a solution to my family's mounting debt? A year earlier, I'd worked for a short while in a gift shop that had the cutest "goldfish soaps." Christmas 2002 approached and I decided to make some soap for my children's classmates and teachers, a cost-effective way to make gifts. My first attempts in my kitchen were less than perfect but each batch showed improvement and I made baskets of goodies for everyone that Christmas. After the holiday gift giving, it wasn't long before people starting asking me about my soaps as unique holiday gifts. My dear high school best girlfriend, also named Dawn, called with a supportive idea: she had signed me up for a local craft show—to show off of my soaps! I didn't want to go, yet our financial situation was critical. My personal stress level mounted.

You see, I'm a very shy person and didn't like talking in public, let alone leading spontaneous "cold" conversations. These activities made my heart race and palms sweat! Reluctantly, I joined my girlfriend and, to my surprise, I out-sold everyone. The very next weekend another girlfriend reserved an antique show table and asked me to sell her antiques while she played the harp for an upcoming show. To sweeten her request, she invited me to bring a tray of my soaps. I went again, reluctantly, and once again out-sold everyone around me.

Mentor Moment
"Life begins at the end of your comfort zone."
~ Larry Wingett

The thought crossed my mind—I had SOMEthing, something special. With only two soap designs (at the time), the very next week I took the soaps to my daughter's Christmas party where one of the teachers gave me the name of a man at the Atlanta Merchandise Mart. It took all the courage I could muster to pick up the phone and call him—yet I did! Come to find out he owned the largest children's showroom at the mart. I called and introduced myself to him. He told me to come on up and show him my product. I quickly got in the car with my basket of soap and off I went. I was so nervous I could hardly breathe. It took me less than an hour to get there. I looked the best I could but knew my weight did not present my true self.

Unfortunately, we live in a world where appearances matter. He really liked my product and began to pace the floor back and forth looking at it and talking to his secretary, more pacing, more talking. I could barely stand it. He finally came back and said he really liked my product but he could not sell only two items. He said I would need a whole line of soap designs. This was news to me. I did not fully understand and I left devastated. I finally got in my car and cried all the way home. I always take everything really seriously and personally. This is something that I try to work on but it comes back on occasion and still gets me. By the time I arrived home I realized I had two choices: quit or take his advice and get a larger line of products.

My mind swam with ideas. That man really motivated me and I soon designed more styles of soaps. I felt I had a good assortment, but before I gave him 15% of all my sales, I thought I would try to sell it on my own first. I was afraid to do a trade show in Atlanta because they felt overwhelming, they were so large. I felt I wasn't ready for that. I decided to do my first trade show in Orlando, Florida. My husband stayed home with the kids and I loaded my soap and my parents in our old suburban and off we went. We had first set up a mock booth in our living room and had worked on it for weeks. When I look back on that first show, I realize we made a lot of mistakes, but we got a lot right also. I still do a lot of things now that I did at the very first show. There will be more on doing trade shows in Chapter 11: Tradeshows.

As I look back I really didn't do too badly at that first show. To me this was the birth of Clearly Fun Soap. I came home with orders to fill. I was so excited. One thing I always try to do is to learn from everyone around me. I was fortunate that I was across from someone at this first show whom I call the *Barracuda*, one of my "path-crossers"! I believe he could sell dirt and be good at it. I was fascinated, and took in all his techniques—how he greeted people, where he stood, everything. I still do a lot of this to this day. I love to learn and so I try to pick everyone's brain around me at every show. I have made dear new friends this way. I ask them what shows they like best, how they got into business, etc. I never ask their sources because this is not a good idea. People can be funny about giving out that kind of information. You can learn a lot by observing. This is also how I met my business mentor. There will be more on that later. I remember being so nervous at my first show. I felt like a fish out of water. It will only take a couple of shows before it seems like you've been doing it a lifetime. Don't be afraid to ask questions. This is how you learn.

There is a tradeshow for just about everything (Research on-line in your own product field. As I see it, you simply must be well-researched in your market, which will lead you to the best tradeshows for your business. Be prepared. They are expensive, though they are worth the networking and exposure, to be sure. Plus, you find out pronto if you truly have a marketable product. There are willing and highly capable buyers at these shows, so if your product sells, or doesn't, you know.

In your research, check out the photos from previous trade shows. You will need a professional presence—a "booth" with product samples and an appealing display. Dress well. Smile often and let your passion for your invention shine through ALL THE TIME. That sells people, too!

Mentor Moment

• *The way to compete with the big boys is to have a break-through product AND be smarter, faster and more efficient.*

• *Create a systematic bill statement process starting less than 30 days out and ask for due dates 30 days from the order. Make sure you get your money. I won't begin to tell you how much bad debt we have had over the years. I could retire on it I'm sure! Remember the small guys (smaller businesses) will take you just as quickly as the big ones. Your business plan and billing systems have to be your priority. A clear and concise business plan—even a two-page short outline is needed to secure loans.*

• *If your largest bills do not get paid on time, it is best to have a collection agency in the wings. You pay a percentage to them from what they collect and it is a last resort. However, if you don't feel they'll ever pay you (60-90 days, three billing statements later) contact a previously arranged collection agency. Do not let things go. It is best to get most of your invoiced money than none at all.*

Mentor Moment

"Successful businesses start from passion. The passion may be creative, such as inventing a product that you love. Passion may be within the very activity of 'conducting business', with an inner excitement for bringing something new into the world. Examine yourself and your idea. Tap into that entrepreneurial spirit that will fuel your longest days and most challenging weeks."

~ D. Dallaire

advice revised from entrepreneur.com

Chapter 2
PASSION, PERSISTENCE
FOR YOUR PRODUCT OR SERVICE

For any project or business to be successful, you will first have to have a passion for what you are doing. This is essential not only for longevity but you will need this passion to carry you on the days when that's all you have left. When you have passion for what you are doing, you will live, eat and sleep it. Your passion will enable you to jump out of bed at 3A.M. with new ideas to write down and get started on. Your passion will become your energy. It will have you up and going early in the morning knowing exactly what you want to accomplish in the days ahead. It will make coffee or diet coke an afterthought and not a need. Your passion will be your new caffeine. There will even be days when this is not enough and you will have to lean on sheer determination to make it.

Every business has a honeymoon phase. This is a great part of starting a business. It's fun, exciting—and makes you feel alive! This is a time when there are more ideas in your head than you know where to place them. Balance is the key. Taking time to simply work hard and move forward will calm those feelings. Taking even one five-minute break every hour to sit in the sun or do some jumping jacks will balance these "I'm drowning!" feelings. Sure, you want to make every day feel like a honeymoon even when it is not because fundamentally you love your idea. You love creating and being successful as a dreammaker. Make absolutely certain that you like what you are doing or it will turn into *work* instead of *work+play*. It could then feel like a very long, hard journey. You must realize that this will be more work than you can probably imagine. I cannot begin to fathom the hours that I logged, especially in the early part of my business. However, sometimes the hours will feel like only minutes when you have passion for your product and you're doing what you want and love to do. I am still amazed at how long it takes to make even small changes. Sometimes, it's hours and days or even weeks just to make one small change. Love what you do and do what you love but be prepared to WORK, WORK, WORK. With passion, even the work will be enjoyable and the work will be fun, and fun is passion. I have this and you should, too. Business skills can be learned, passion cannot. While passion is essential, it is not enough. You will still have to have customers who want to buy your product. You will have to be smart, resourceful and learn your business skills early.

One of the skills you will have to learn is *persistence*. Being persistent is easy when you believe in your product and yourself. With any business or walk of life there are times when you have to be determined to make it work. This is one of my favorite lessons that I've learned. When my business was very busy and we had more on our plates than it seemed we could handle my mentor said to me, "Go get more business." I could not understand this when it seemed I needed to be working on the orders I had. I knew that I had hired others to do the production and it was my job to get the orders, but we were so busy. I could not see the need to acquire more business when we were swamped. This seemed completely foreign to me until one day the orders were completed and there I sat with twelve full-time employees and no orders. That's when it hit me…and "Go get more accounts!" had a whole new meaning. I should *not* have been helping tie and prepare the orders; my time was better spent bringing in more business. No orders means no money coming in. No money coming in means not being able to pay rent, payroll, bills, etc. When you are the leader of the company, your job is to lead. This comes with great responsibility. It isn't all about you; others are counting on you to do your job so they, in fact, continue having theirs.

An example of being persistent was when I was trying to call on a large corporation in Atlanta. I wanted to make an appointment to show them my products. I called and got the buyer's name and voicemail. I left several messages, but no reply. Two days later I called and left another message stating I was going to be in Atlanta and would like to make an appointment to see her. Again, no reply. At that point I thought it was hopeless. However, being persistent, which I was beginning to learn, I decided just to show up with my samples—a "cold call". This was way out of my comfort zone, but by this time I knew that being persistent was the only chance I had. I had nothing to lose and everything to gain. Though I still had a million excuses why this day would not be the best day to go, I decided to go anyway.

When I got there, the buyer's office was heavily guarded and they would not let me in. I explained my plight to the security guard, but to no avail. He did let me know that I could go a few streets over to their shipping and receiving warehouse and have the samples delivered from there. I did this and they said the buyer would have them in less than an hour. As I pulled away I was sure I would never get any response. The next day I called to follow up and left a message. Again, no reply. It is important when you are persistent to follow up daily until you get a response. You have to believe in your product and be confident that making the right calls like this will develop into business. But again there was no reply.

The next time I called I tried to make them feel bad for not calling me back. I wasn't harsh, but I did plead and say I wanted to just make sure they had received my samples. Five minutes later the buyer called me back to say she loved them and had sent them over to licensing and I would hear back in a week. I couldn't believe it. I was so excited. In my recent past, I would have quit long before this, but this is a good example of being persistent. I try never to be rude, yet sometimes sheer determination can get you things you never dreamed possible. So get out there and hit the phone and the road and most of all, BE PERSISTENT and especially, follow up.

Another example of this is trying and trying to get an appointment with a large retail buyer. This was a well-known New York based international company. I created customized samples and shipped them. I called and continued calling several times for four months before obtaining an appointment.

Not all products or services will have what it takes to make it. You must research and test your product in the marketplace to see if it has what it takes to go all the way. Some people are fortunate and just happen upon this, but most have to try many times to get the right product or idea to market. One idea I had before CFS was a children's kitchen set called "Sarah Girl." I spent many months and finally came to the realization that it would not be profitable. It cost too much to make for what I could charge. I still have a file in my drawer with all the work I did, and my daughter has a very expensive children's kitchen set to hopefully pass on to her daughter someday. There were many more before this, so don't be discouraged if your first, second, or even more ideas don't succeed. When the time is right and the product is excellent and marketable, it will fall into place.

One thing that I have lacked is confidence. Some of this lack of confidence came from being a very shy child. While I was not overweight as a child, I spent most of my adult life struggling with my weight. In time even a person who used to have self confidence can have it eaten away. I hated myself for being overweight. I knew I was not my best and this only stressed me more. Whatever your reasons, remember you can overcome. I'm living proof of this. As a shy person, it was only passion for my product and the desire to feed my family that allowed me to begin to stand up and sell my product. Now when I give a speech or sell my product at a trade show I will hear myself talking. I can hardly believe it's me doing that. It's amazing what a little age and determination can do to even this very shy girl from the South. Many times it was only the fact that I had to make money or lose everything that kept me going. I have often wondered how people who do not need the money actually make it. I had no choice but to succeed. I am not saying that you can't make it if you don't need the money, but in my case it was the only thing many times that drove me on—that, along with passion for my product, is still the driving force years later.

Most entrepreneurs are creative people but you will also need a lot of energy to go along with this. Stay healthy, keep balance between your business life and family and friends time. It takes a tremendous amount of energy to start and grow a business. Always remember to keep fresh, rejuvenate yourself, stay focused on what you love about your product line and keep PASSION, PERSISTENCE, and a PRODUCT that you believe in alive deep within yourself!

Mentor Moment

Don't just accept charge backs and partial payments when you have delivered goods. Often times a company's way of doing business is to prolong payment of their POs (purchase orders) and invoices. Don't let them get away with that. Get paid. Keep after the bills. Pennies make dollars, which add up to millions. Be diligent in this regard.

Chapter 3
GETTING STARTED...
...and also being a Mother

When I began CFS, one of my main objectives was to be a stay-at-home mom, since my children were in elementary school and needed me, especially when they got home from school and throughout the summers. This objective worked for a short time, because the business was in our home. Then, joyfully, the business developed and we were bursting at the seams!

This is when a personal conflict arose in me because I could no longer stay at home. Sometimes I felt as if I were barely "mom-ing" at all. Please consider carefully your family life as you move forward. This is where a timeline and specific business plan with due dates and your family life are all taken into consideration. Be prepared to shift and change if—or rather when—your product takes off.

One of my favorite passages from the book *It's Called Work for a Reason*, by Larry Wingett, shown before this chapter, moves me still. "Everything comes at a price, even doing nothing." Let me say that again—everything comes with a price. What price are you willing to pay? In addition, remember doing nothing comes at a price.

I began CFS when my youngest child was in kindergarten, and my oldest in the fourth grade, so I was able to stay home with my children during these early years. And now, I see that my children have picked many, many business-making tips and approaches. Even though they say they do not remember the first years, I see how they think now and it is very *entrepreneur-like*. So when/ if you do move to an out-of-home location, know that showing your children that you make mistakes, you learn along the way—these are all wonderful apprenticeships for their careers and businesses later in life. It's all good, as my son would say!

A first thing you will need is a product or service that sells. No one wants to be told they "need" something. Everyone wants to feel that they "want and desire" something. You must feel that your product or service must sell FUN, SECURITY, CONTENTMENT or whatever name you give it. Make sure your product idea delights others; don't tell them they need anything. When you tell someone they "need", their first reaction is NO I don't need anything. What they really need is only air and water.

That said, now you sell them your idea and what it will make them feel like once they have purchased it. In my case it's FUN. Clearly Fun Soap, sell FUN! Once you have your product or service it's time to give your new company a name. I cannot emphasize how important this is. This is the part of your business where you will want to get as much feedback as possible from friends and family. I had originally wanted the name GOOD CLEAN FUN. This simply appeals to EVERYONE. I discovered this name was already taken. A friend of mine helped me come up with the name. This process may take awhile. Once you have your name you need to trademark it.

Make sure the name is right and you are serious about starting a business. It will cost you some money to trademark your name but you need to do this to continue. You would hate to do all the work that you will do over the next months and years and not have your name protected. Your business is your name, so invest in it. You can register your name yourself at www.uspto.gov or you can call 1-800-786-9199. The cost will vary depending on your application type but will probably cost between $275 and $375. It will take approximately three weeks to receive your receipt of registration and then up to a year to be certified if there are no issues. This will take some time but will be well worth the effort. Name recognition is everything. Protect your brand (name). Or you can pay an attorney to do it for you. I'm not the most computer savvy person but I was able to do this online. There is also a maintenance fee and other charges. You can read the details when you go to the web site.

After your name is protected you need to secure a web site. Keep it simple. This may even affect the name of your company so do your research early on. I started my first web site with my neighbor's help. This may be an economical way to start, but unless they are super talented, you will at some point need your web site done professionally. After being in business for almost four years it was time for me to change. This is one area I believe you get what you pay for. Check out a lot of web sites and write down which ones you like and why. When you meet with your web designer you can convey these ideas to them. At some point, after your business becomes more established, you can hire a firm that will help you with web design, brochures, logos, catalogs, etc. This will allow you to become professional and have a uniformed look. In order to attract the "big buyers" you will need to be professional. As you're getting started keep this in the back of your mind and make it your goal to work at this. Your web site will also need an "About Us" page as well as a "Company History" page. You may not feel like you have much to say in the beginning but remember that people love to hear how you got started and your goals. We all have an entrepreneur lurking within and we all like to see how someone actually has done what we've all thought about doing. It doesn't have to be long but it does need to be interesting.

Depending on your budget, as you grow you will need a Certified Public Accountant (CPA) and an attorney. These professionals are experts. Hiring them, even if for only a few hours to begin with, can and will save you so much time as you refine your incorporation type, business plans, timelines 2, 3, 4 years out. They will interview you, and you will interview them. Don't wait around for just their advice; ask friends, business associates, and interview three or more. Take notes on what they advise. You may take their advice or even hire others for specific information in the future. It's best to have done your homework and know who is there when the need arises. Like a great maintenance plan, professionals such as CPAs, attorneys and bankers will help a solid business foundation set-up. And it is good business practice building local and regional trust. When you are in rapid growth their expertise is what will boost your business, rather than your thinking you have to do it all. There will be more on this in a later chapter.

Keep in mind, however, that it is your company. Use your head. Weigh the advice. Research your field more.

Always research and make it a continual practice. Think about your Code of Ethics and how you wish to operate. If a professional does not fit into your ethics, do not force that relationship. Let them go and seek to align with others with your same outlook on business practices. Post this Code of Ethics and Mission Statements from your corporate papers, so everyone who works with you knows them and can state them easily. Answer questions like: What do you wish your company to stand for?

YOUR BRAND

Your brand is who you are and what you make. It is your name in the world. Always protect it. It is your baby! For your business to become a household name, and therefore become valuable, you have to have a brand. If your goal is to sell your business, then this becomes even more important. When someone is buying a business one of the things they are buying is your brand. So grow it, nurture it, and protect it.

What do I mean by protect it? First, trademark and/or servicemark your company and logo and secondly watch your quality. When you grow and take on more employees this will become of utmost importance. You will always make sure the quality is up to your standards. The challenge is to convey this to someone else. Take the time to train your employees in the beginning. This is better known as *quality control*. Fortunately there are a lot of good people out there who, once trained properly, will do a good job for you—lead by example. Once your business begins to grow and you hire people to help you then your job description will change. You will no longer be making the product; your job will be to sell so you can pay the people you've hired. This was a hard transition for me. When you've been the one doing everything for so long it's difficult to relinquish control in this area. But don't worry because when the time comes you will have no choice, if you want to grow. Your job description will change many times during the course of your business life. It's important to be flexible and keep your ultimate goals, whatever they may be, in mind. There was a time when I poured, bagged, tied, sold, shipped, billed, and collected payments. Countless nights I sat in bed watching TV while tying my soaps. Back then, I never would have believed I would hire a whole team of *tyers*! ENJOY every aspect of your business as you are growing and expanding wisely. It's truly fun if you step back and reflect as you go.

Life is short. Enjoy the ride.

About two years ago I went on a white water rafting trip that became a *barometer* for my life, especially my business life. At the beginning of the trip it was exhilarating, exciting and pure fun. It wasn't long before we were stuck on some rocks, and I mean really stuck. I had the bright idea to get out and push. I got out and pushed the raft loose, and it took off without me. I slipped and under the rapids I went. When I came up I was moving quickly down the rapids with my life passing before me and my friends and daughter were moving farther away from me in the raft. I really didn't know if I would drown or not. I decided not to panic but to remain calm. This was a much better decision than the one I previously made, which was to get out and push. My friends were able to get the raft over to the side. They pulled me back in the raft safely. My pride was tarnished, yet was I ever glad to be back in that raft. No matter how many more times we became stuck, and there were many, I never got out of the raft again. Sometimes it was calm and other times it was turbulent. At times we went down the river backwards and sometimes forward but we were always moving toward our goal, which was finishing the river. I have thought often about this trip and how it is such an example of my life and especially my business life.

Some lessons I've learned:
- Stay in the raft.
- Don't give up.
- Don't panic, remain calm.
- You don't always have control but keep moving in the right direction.
- Plan your journey, but be flexible. (I never imagined I would own a soap business.)
- If you fall out of the raft, hopefully you will have friends to pull you back in.
- Enjoy the scenery.

GETTING STARTED CHECKLIST
- Name your business
- Search it out
- Register – Trademark and/or Servicemark, product or service dependent
- Get Business License
- Incorporate now or when?
- Secure your web site
- Checking Account, start-up funds, limit this in a first budget (It's great if you have money, but I began with only $20!)

- Hire an Accountant/Bookkeeper/CPA
- Hire an attorney
- Logo, slogan, theme to your line
- Make a plan
- Create a beginning "Code of Ethics"
- Stay organized
- Office space? In-home or how much overhead can you afford during first production; just use your garage?
- Later on, try a financial advisor – at the start pick peoples' brains!
- Start interviewing for employees, part-time to see how they work with you

---

Mentor Moment

From the start, put healthy eating and exercise in your plan. Make a permanent appointment in your planner for them. Stick to it. When stress is high and things aren't going your way, you will still feel good physically and will handle your business better.

Mentor Moment

Scenario: your shipping labels do not have the required information. The labels are actually wrong. Try spray painting the old and slap on new labels. This doesn't hold up shipment as much as taking off the old labels or re-packing.

Chapter 4
IMPORTING and EXPORTING
and DOMESTIC SHIPPING

Part of expanding your line to keep your customers interested may include importing at some point. Importing and Exporting is not as difficult as it sounds. There are, however, some precautions you will need to take.

IMPORTING

As with any business, there are risks. It is important that you try to make sure you are importing from a reputable company. Having a reliable agent will help you in this area. There are a lot of unethical companies out there and you need to do your best to make sure you are working with a legitimate company, someone you feel you can trust. My first experience importing was from China. If you are importing from China you will need to take into account the Chinese New Year (Date of each new year sometime in February). If you are dealing with them during this special holiday time it can delay your shipment up to three weeks. Another thing you need to be prepared for is for your shipment to get delayed by customs. I recently had a shipment pulled. They did what's called a *Devan*, this is where your shipment is x-rayed and taken to an exam room. If all goes well it may only delay it a few days, but it could cause up to a month delay.

Once you establish a repertoire with the importing company, its culture and the product you want to import, you will deal with them mainly through emails. There will normally be someone in their company who speaks English. However, you should set a company goal to try and deal with the actual sales person or owner.

Fortunately, English is the pervasive international language of business and the majority of companies that export to the United States will have someone available to help you communicate. Generally, overseas companies will have at least a five thousand dollar wholesale order minimum. Some may require a full container load (FCL). A standard full container load is 40'L x 8.5' x 8'W. You normally buy in kilos as opposed to pounds (1kg = 2.2046 lbs). You do not have to start out buying FCLs. Many companies or agents will allow you to do what's called a LCL, Less than a Container Load. The price of your product may be slightly higher if you buy LCL but it's the best way to start. You have to be careful always to control your inventory. You don't want all your money tied up in slow moving inventory. In the chapter on my mistakes I will tell you how I did this early on and almost didn't recover. For now let me just tell you that I have enough grasshopper toys to sink a ship. It's best, to begin with, only to purchase the items you know sell really well. Start by requesting a quote on the items you are purchasing and samples. You do not have to accept the first quote they give you. Give negotiating a lower price a chance. Similar to buying a car, never accept the first offer. It's the same with business. Most overseas companies expect this. Price bottom lines may go lower and frequently do. They will ask for their money up front, yet try to negotiate terms such as CAD (cash against documents) and/or 80% payment upfront, 20% after arrival and inspection of goods. I started out having to pay 50% at the time I ordered and 50% when it was ready to ship. After gaining their trust and you theirs we now pay 40% up front and the remaining 60% upon delivery. To pay said money, most companies normally will require you to go through a bank. The best way is to actually get full terms, and it never hurts to ask for them. However, with importing, this normally will not happen until you develop a strong relationship with the company in which you are dealing. They feel the same risk as you do, if they are reliable. If you can negotiate terms, it will help to protect you so that if the goods do not arrive as anticipated, you have some recourse and may not have to pay at all. This is not necessarily good because then you do not have your product. This is really even worse. Knowing who you are dealing with is paramount for these reasons. Usually it is half of the invoice to get started and the final half before shipment.

To wire the money you will need to go through a bank. You will need to get an international wire transfer form from your bank. Then you have to get their bank account with routing numbers information, and the exact name and address of the exporter's bank. You have to go to your bank with this information and they will help you wire the funds. There is a bank fee for this process and I have found that you may create "repetitive wire-transfers process" in advance, which can be called-in from your telephone once all of the regular client information is secured at your bank. Ask for an appointment with your banker and explain your business needs. Most banks are eager to have regular business customers.

When I finally found a product that I wanted to import, my international importing journey began. I spent countless hours on the Internet trying to figure out how it all worked. After I had ordered my product and it was about ready to ship, panic began to set in. How would I get it to my warehouse?

Fortunately, I am always meeting new people and the first day of a trade show, I mentioned to a colleague that I was trying to import product from China. To my amazement, this person was familiar with importation and a new advisor relationship quickly developed. He said he would help me if I'd send him the exact specifications. My stress eased, and confusion soon dissipated when my new advisor set me right. I listened to every bit of sound advice, quite simply because I knew nothing about this arena, other than my Internet research. He even volunteered to take care of my importing after that. While I was relieved and knew help was on the way, I didn't want to just *have it done for me* because my personal approach is always to learn how to do it myself. So I set out to learn everything I could with the help of this colleague and the importer directly. I now know a concise, tried-and-true way to clear my goods through customs once they arrive stateside. I was advised to find a "customer house broker" who was in the business of entering and clearing goods when they arrive.

Brokers will need the following in sets of three: ORIGINAL BILLS OF LADING, COMMERCIAL INVOICES, and PROFORMA INVOICES. Sometimes they will need a FORM A, which is a Certificate of Origin.

You have to request this from the exporting company and have it sent to you, probably through Federal Express

(FedEx). After you receive this, you keep one copy for yourself and send the other two on to your broker. I was fortunate that I was able to use the same customs house broker that this importer-now-mentor used. He was nice enough to share this information with me. A customs house broker can be found in most major United States cities.

Once all the paperwork has been sent to the broker, he starts entering and clearing the goods. The goods cannot be shipped to my warehouse until they have been cleared and approved by our government. Sometimes there are additional fees such as *duty*. It all depends on what you are importing. You will want to shop around not only for the best price, but one that can help you get your particular product through customs. For me it was that easy. The broker tracks the shipment, unloads it in a warehouse and has it repacked and shipped to you. It is really not that hard as long as you have the right people to help you. An average shipment is on the water for thirty days, depending on what country is shipping it and what port it is going to. Then you have to allow another 7-10 days for the goods to arrive to you. This is, of course, if there are no glitches getting it though customs. I thought I had to understand customs rules and regulations. I spent so much time trying to read government websites, etc. This is where a good broker comes in and is worth the fee that they charge. They do this all the time and are familiar with the customs rules and regulations.

The exporting company will request your shipping marks, such as the samples below:

Front
CLEARLY FUN SOAP
P.I. NO. PI-2849
ITEM NO: (Exporter's item no.)
MADE IN CHINA
C/NO. 1-UP   (Total cartons)

Side Mark
QTY. PCS   (Total qty per item)
NW: KGS   (Net weight)
GW: KGS   (Gross weight)
MEAS._____x_____x_____CM

EXPORTING

Exporting is very different from importing. On the whole, you will be dealing with American-based companies. The first things you need to know are the product quantity, number of containers, total weight, pallet dimensions, and destination. It takes time, but you have to call many companies for shipping quotes. It is vital that you know the current rates because there are vast differences. This diligent calling can save thousands of dollars.

Once your order is complete and you are confident about the company handling your goods, they will require form-sets of three, as above, only of packing slips and/ or invoices. From there, they will handle the rest: scheduling pick-up and providing tracking and confirmation to get your shipment to its final destination. Every country has unique requirements, but the company that exports will be able to show you the way.

DOMESTIC SHIPPING

One of my favorite web sites is www.freightquote.com. You can register free on this web site and do all your tractor trailer shipping this way. It's a great way to check pricing also. However, at some point when you begin to ship pallets on a regular basis you will want to establish a relationship with a large trucking company (i.e. Yellow, Old Dominion, Roadway, etc.) The reason for this is that they can be very accommodating if you get in a bind. Establishing a relationship with trucking companies can also offer discounts in importing. Let them know you also check freightquote. This keeps them in check and you can make sure you are getting the best rate whether you or your customer is paying. When the customer pays it's called COLLECT. When you are paying it's called PREPAID. Again, just like in overseas shipping you will need documents, just not 3 copies of everything. Do not send any shipments out your door without a BOL (Bill of Lading). You can make your own or get them from the trucking company. Make sure the driver signs it and attaches his bar code label to your copy so you have proof they picked it up. The bar code stickers they apply are your tracking numbers. Believe it or not, shipments get lost and your BOL is your record that it left your dock and was accounted for.

As for regular everyday box shipments, I am a die-hard UPS fan. I have used them since the beginning and they are very reliable. They provide you the software you need and rent you a label printer for a small fee. They are easy to use. There is a lot of competition in this arena so you will want to do your research and decide which company you'd like to use. You can set up a driver schedule. When I first committed to having a driver come every day, I was worried we wouldn't have enough to ship. I don't think we've ever had a day since that we haven't had something to ship. In the beginning I would drive to Office Depot every day and ship from there. Once you get an account established it will save you not only time but money. Once you begin to ship regularly you will want to have the company come to you. Only after we began to cause a scene daily from shipping so much did a UPS driver finally tell me we needed to have the truck come to our home. I felt so grownup when they finally came every day!

> **Mentor Moments: Phrases to know about.**
> Research these and set-up before your first major international shipment, if you wish to be a global company:
> - Customs House Broker
> - Forwarder/Shipping Company
> - Port of Discharge
> - Bill of Lading
> - Chinese New Year, important to know this date
> - Booking a vessel for shipment (ship)

If a shipper doesn't deliver in the time contracted, insist on air flight to meet your own delivery goals. This creates a strong reputation for expecting your shipping agreements to be fulfilled in a timely manner—no exceptions. It is YOUR BRAND and YOUR REPUTATION that is on the line for every order.

> **Mentor Moment**
> Remember to get a customs broker and LET THEM GUIDE YOU. You do not need to spend time outside your own product business to know every aspect of customs and the various international rules. That is their job. Your job is to develop and sell products and refine your services.

Chapter 5
PUBLIC RELATIONS

Are public relations (PR) necessary? YES!

Public relations materials are a cost-effective way to promote your business. As a matter of fact, "PR" often costs nothing, yet is much more than simply sending out a press release via broadcast email or hardcopy. PR embraces numerous chances to increase your company's visibility, while gaining credibility—a powerful sales tool. However, a master plan must be crafted. Planning with a specific set of goals and objectives will make your story newsworthy and thus your company better known. Below are some highly effective guidelines.

Remember, the more interesting your company's story the more interest you generate and the more press/media coverage you earn. It's high-end advertising you just can't buy. Often, human interest background material catapults into fabulously free publicity worth hundreds and even thousands of dollars. A unique story will grasp readers and viewers and can have a dramatic impact on your present and potential clients and customers. Keep in mind that all the PR you receive will also need to go on your web site. It's an effective means of promotion to your captive markets and further substantiates your market position in your field.

PR and *brandname recognition* is your chance to develop your brand—such as Kleenex instead of just saying tissues. We all have to start somewhere and invest some start-up money on this valuable presence in the hands of businesses and people. Be creative and learn from other PR pieces in your field that move you. Feel the paper, look at the color options and have fun with it.

I recently went to what was called a "Media Event" in New York City. This is where you pay and set up a table of your product. Then magazine editors come by and look at your table and decide if they would like to feature you in their magazine. Still uncertain how it went on the magazine feature part, I did end up on CNBC's show "The Big Idea" with Donny Deutsch. What a blast! I flew to New York and a limousine driver was there waiting for me, holding one of those little signs with my name on it. How cool! I frequently see these signs, but never before with my name on it. The next morning the hotel clerk called my room and said, "Mrs. Dallaire, your driver is here waiting whenever you're ready." I had to ask her to repeat this since I've never had anyone call and say that to me. In my world I hear things like, "Hurry, Mom", or "I'll be late for school." It was truly a fun time and I tried to enjoy every moment of it. At the media event I passed out a press kit and sample of the soap to everyone who showed interest.

Public Relations Press Kit Items Recommended:

- Short (1-2 page) fact sheet describing your products or services, your history, key personnel, the number of employees, your location(s), sales, the number of products, the number of customers and any other interesting and unique-to-you facts you might want to include. Please include phone numbers, even after-hours phone numbers if available.

• Biography of key individuals such as partners, private investors (if they wish this info out there), especially with expertise pertaining to your product line.

• List of products and services, especially unique niches your company provides.

• Photographs and displays of products or services, facility and key personnel.

• Cover letter—reminder: more is not necessarily better. Press people have a lot of information to sort through; brevity with high interest in your cover letter is more effective than too much detail.

• Copies of any previous publications (magazines, newspapers, etc.). The longer you are at this the more of this you will get. All of it helps to give you credibility, name recognition and generate an enthusiasm for you and your product.

I was recently selected as "Small Business Person of the Year" for the state of Georgia. It is truly an honor and will lend credibility to me and my product. It will go in my press kit as well as on the cover of my book. Can you see how one thing leads to another? So use every opportunity to its fullest. Besides that, it's fun and it gives you a chance to meet new and interesting people as well as test yourself. It really pays to be a "Woman in Business". Let's show them what we're made of!!

Let your media kit work for you. Use it for recruiting, getting loans, and attracting investors.

CLEARLY FUN SOAP'S FIRST!

What a thrill it was when my first newspaper article was published. It was a great full-color front page article in the business section with several pictures. The young reporter who interviewed me did a great job detailing the history, product, growth, and even promoted this yet unpublished book! Hot off the press, I copied and quickly used this article to supplement my PR packets and press kits, thus increasing public presence. Through quick thinking, I sent newspaper copies to potential customers with product samples, as well as to other newspapers in the region.

A side-effect of this first large-scale press coverage was that it boosted our busy staff's morale! Even though it was in a small-town paper, the press exposure still offered a substantial chance for new growth. Of course, more public exposure can lead to some interesting phone calls. An example of this was when a sales broker called with interest in placing my product in big-name chain stores. It also produced some crazy calls like, "Did you used to work at K-mart?" and "Don't you have a sister or brother who went to...high school?" It was from this same article that I ended up on QVC. A local man saw it and sent it to a friend of his in Tennessee who brokers products for QVC. He called me and introduced himself and a business friendship quickly developed. My QVC broker and I have been through a lot to get the product on air. When you begin to get your name out there you just never know where it will take you. Be ready for the ride.

"Divine Intervention" twice, thrice and more!

What do you call a coincidence that just bowls you over because it is so right and good for you or your company? Fate? Luck? Synchronicity? Like-hearts think alike? Only six degrees of separation? Destiny? I have termed some happenstances in my life as "Divine Intervention" and this little event is a prime example of how saying yes can lead to many happy returns:

The term "Public Relations" is, after all, about relationships. Your bank account of assets in business and in life is filled with concrete, dependable, trustful relationships with suppliers, clients, professionals, and advisors. During the product shows, I frequently reach out and meet as many people as possible, telling them about my business and hoping they will remember my products and that they will sell more! An important vendor I befriended ended up challenging me in a way that turned into the biggest *ah-ha* moment of my life.

PUBLIC APPEARANCES

Recently I was asked to join in an entrepreneurial luncheon as a keynote speaker. I accepted, knowing it would push me way past my comfort zone. I did it and it was okay. I wasn't great from my inner point of view, but I got a lot of good feedback. People were inspired. I am pleased about that; helping even one person is a super feeling. Within two days, I received several new orders from that group!!

I learned that paying attention to your local business colleagues is excellent business practice. I never realized how valuable it can be for my personal growth and also, some extra sales sure don't hurt! In addition, it is terrific business practice to support your community by becoming a member of civic and business organizations. Everyone wins and you never know when a relationship could really boost your business.

I have now made many more speeches. It's still not my favorite thing to do, but it's important, in order to give back to the community at large and to keep my brand and my business out there. I have learned to enjoy the question and answer time at the end of my speech and I especially like speaking to young business students. I doubt I'll ever be a great speaker, but I do it anyway. I cannot believe that I am in a place in my life where this is necessary, but it is. Be willing to do whatever it takes and I know you will succeed!

A Public Relations chain reaction:
- Announce you have a new business
- Newspaper article write up in local paper
- Broker for QVC sees article
- QVC brings more credibility
- Larger newspaper article written
- Scoop magazine does cover story

- Give lots of speeches
- Nominated Small Business Person of the year
- Selected Small Business Person of the year
- Appear on CNBC show
- Larger stores become more interested
- Revenues Grow

Everyone's PR adventure will be different. I left out many details but you can see how one thing leads to another. You want to create an exciting buzz about you and your business. Be able to back it up with a good product and good customer service. The bottom line is, *just do it* and enjoy it!

Mentor Moments
- Have something to say. Have something to sell.
- Replication Saves Time—Students are Qualified
- Keep copies of everything, including your press. It saves time if you re-use articles.
- Try paying a college journalism major $50 per article and $50 for each newspaper or magazine in which the article is published. Money well spent and you give a qualified person some real apprenticeship experience.
- Try a Warehouse Sale—it is great Local PR!
- Hold a leftover or old inventory sale. Advertise in the paper. Make it an event with a raffle or lottery for a prize (a product every month for six months, etc.). This creates room in your warehouse and great local relationships.

Chapter 6
THE "OTHER" CHALLENGE –
My Health and Weight Loss Story

This is the most difficult part of my life to write about and yet the one for which I have the most passion. I don't really understand the *whys* and *why nots* as to my weight gain. I have done lots of soul searching and have many theories, some of which will show up in other chapters. While I have managed to lose 120+ pounds and so far have kept it off, I by no means profess to be an expert or have all the answers. I do believe we can all lose weight the same way. It's simply how much you put in your mouth and how much you exercise. I know this is not pleasant to hear. The difficult part is what motivates each person to lose weight and keep being motivated through life's trials and tribulations. I believe this is different for each person.

This is what no one can figure out, and the reason the diet industry is a multi-billion dollar industry. There are many diets that help you lose weight, but it's the motivation to get started and stick with it that can't be fixed by a diet. This has to come from within. I know it can be done no matter how hopeless you may feel. I was sure I was destined to be fat and had truly given up hope. I thought it was my lot in life to have fat genes and I would most likely die an early death because of my bad eating habits. I was never the kind of person who was comfortable being overweight. I was obsessed with it day and night. I let it affect every area of my life.

I looked so bad in whatever I wore that I no longer tried. I remember once I was shopping at Filene's Dept. Store and was riding down the escalator. I looked in the mirror and saw this very large unattractive woman and, when I realized it was me, I left the store crying. Because of this I rarely would put on make up. I didn't care about my hair and almost never dressed up. My wardrobe consisted of stretchy pants and big shirts. This only added to my misery. I had tried every diet under the sun. In the end I did none of them to lose all this weight. When my time came to lose this weight, I was a veteran dieter and decided I had given enough of my money away. I knew how to lose weight; now I just had to do it.

For me the journey began a year earlier, in January of 2004. I was at the merchandise mart in Atlanta doing a tradeshow. Another exhibitor and I talked during the show about losing weight. We made a wager. Whoever lost the most weight over the next year would take the other one to dinner when we returned the following January. I never told anyone about this bet because I didn't really want to live up to it. The year began to tick by and I would say to myself, "I better start." Then it was September and I'd say again, "I better start." Finally, it was December and I said, "Oh no, it's too late." When the day came to see this exhibitor I was sitting there as big as ever, almost 300 pounds. I was too big to even want to get up. I looked like an elephant sitting on a stool. I kept praying, "Dear God, please don't let him remember we made this bet." As he and his colleague turned the corner he took one look at me and said, "I won." He looked great and there I sat. It was devastating—not that he had said that, but that I had let a whole year go by and done nothing to lose weight. In fact, I probably had gained another 30 lbs. I was so embarrassed and angry with myself.

This was not only a *light bulb* moment for me but a *sledgehammer* moment. I had no excuse for not having at least lost some weight. The show quickly started and I stood there taking orders, but I could think of nothing except how angry I was at myself. Even with this life-shattering feeling, I drove every day to the mart that January, eating a sausage and cheese biscuit with a chocolate bar. I would eat a Philly cheesesteak sandwich with chips and another chocolate bar at lunch, and who knows what I was eating for dinner. I was miserable!!! My husband and I did have a nice dinner with the exhibitor, his wife and colleague. I remember driving to the restaurant that night, hoping no one noticed that my stomach was so large it was touching the steering wheel. I have long legs and always have my seat pushed all the way back. I'll let you imagine this moment and my feelings.

At the end of the five-day show, I asked the exhibitor to make the wager with me again. He was gracious enough to oblige. After all, he had already gotten a nice dinner out of the first bet and the odds were with him to win again. I had so much weight to lose, and yet I knew if I dieted and exercised diligently, I could do it over the next year. There was not a day to lose.

I learned over this next year just how competitive I really am. It amazed even me. I still knew the odds were against me, but that made me only more competitive. I'm a beat-the-odds kind of girl, and you can be, too! I began the next day after our mart show and bet— and I did not cheat for one year!

My keys to weight loss: a reasonable goal, a sensible and healthy diet, imagining, clearly and often, that moment when a trusted friend sees you for the first time in a year. This vision of meeting my colleague walking around the vendor showroom corner in a year—I cannot tell you how this image of the new me in my mind helped me with my new diet and lifestyle change. There were many, many times when I would put down the food in May or July because I knew the choices I made then would affect that meeting moment, and I chose to be healthier and thinner.

Mentor Moment

It's tough at first but if you stick with it (and have a mentor or two or three to share the exercise and experience with) you will get results.

As I said earlier, I am not licensed in any way to tell someone else what to do, but I can share my experience. For me it is truly "mind over body". I had to go to war with my flesh. This is still a daily on-going battle. I had to come to grips with myself and tell my body that it was no longer in charge and from this day forward it was me (my mind and thoughts) that were now in control. You have to be so determined and when your body starts to revolt, which it will do in just a matter of hours, tell yourself—let your inner YOU know—the overeating is all over and you're in charge. Once this takes place and you win the first battles, your habit of eating will weaken and disappear. It will take days and months before the old habit releases you, and yet surprisingly with each battle you win the flesh becomes weaker and your inner self becomes stronger!

Mentor Moment
Throw away your old clothing as you lose weight, so you will never have to wear it again! But save one outfit to compare...that is VERY powerful.

I ate so many salads, and when I thought I couldn't eat another one, I ate another one just so my body knew who was in charge. I was so hungry those first few days but with the encouragement of a friend, I was able to get over this first difficult hurdle. I felt like I was hungry for the first six months. After that, the hunger did subside. I even learned to like the hunger pains. I felt like it meant my diet was working. I visualized a thinning me. And I convinced myself that real misery is when you overeat. That became a far worse feeling than hunger pains. I also knew that I had to be realistic, and that crash dieting would not work, and would only end in failure again. One year was a reasonable goal. I wanted to lose 120 pounds, and that was only ten pounds a month or two-three pounds a week. The first month I lost twenty pounds and then ten every month after. Those first pounds came off quickly but I knew I did not have a day to lose. I can truly say that I did not cheat for one year. I kept my thinner vision of myself clear and constant.

This doesn't mean that I didn't have anything besides salad, but I continually counted calories and never just sat down and let go. I'm sure a lot of those first pounds were water weight. I drank what seemed like gallons of water, especially in the early part of my diet. Having a new, fast-growing business also contributed to my dieting success. I was busy and was not hanging around the refrigerator. I have deemed my refrigerator and pantry as "EVIL"—or at least not healthy places for me to hang-around. When I am home I hear the refrigerator call my name; I just don't answer by eating any more.

When the time came to move the business out of my home it was very difficult, yet looking back I realize how much this helped me lose weight. It was hard for me to be home and have control. It's much easier to be away as far as my diet is concerned. Weekends at home are still a struggle for me and I'm in a constant battle with my mind and body even now. Make no mistake about it, it's hard and it's painful, but it is so well worth it. There is nothing that would make me go back. There is not one bite of food that is worth my giving up my size 8. I can remember thinking I would kiss the ground to fit in a size 12. I never even let myself imagine that I could wear a size 8. Food is so temporary and I realized that the results of overeating can do a lifetime of damage. It's not worth giving up your health, your youth, and your beauty for indulging yourself in food. Everything must be done in moderation.

This was a tough lesson for me. I tend to do everything in the extreme. I admire anyone who can go their whole life and live it with moderation. Unfortunately, you cannot be 130 pounds overweight for as long as I was (over twenty years) and not have some terrible side effects. I lost the weight without surgery, but when I was done I needed surgery to remove the excess skin. I was fortunate that most of my weight was in my middle and I was able to take care of most of it with a tummy tuck. This was major surgery and almost cost me my life. When I began my diet in mid-January I had no plans for having plastic surgery. I only decided on this because the skin from my stomach hung down and was never going back—no matter how much exercise I did. I had some complications with blood clots from the surgery and spent most of November and December in and out of the hospital.

It was a difficult time for my very supportive family, friends, and for me, but I would still do it again to have a flat stomach! This surgery choice is definitely not for everyone and must be well thought out. I had a well-qualified surgeon who did a great job. Unfortunately, no one could foresee the problems with the blood clots. I do recommend that if you've had problems with blood clots in the past and are planning on this surgery to first see a hematologist.

It took me six months and seventy pounds of weight loss before I could even think about exercising. A friend of mine, Danielle, encouraged me to go to *Curves*. I was so out of shape. When I was young I was athletic, but twenty years of neglect had taken its toll. *Curves* was the perfect solution for me. When I first arrived I was skeptical, yet I was determined, had a supportive friend and stuck with it. I went 3-5 times a week and after about two months I began to see a difference. I felt stronger and stronger and I did this until I had my surgery. The ladies there were so encouraging and really cheered me on. After I recovered from my surgery, I wanted to do more than *Curves* and joined our local gym. I go faithfully, at least five days a week. With the encouragement of a friend I get up at 6A.M. every morning and workout before work. I have never felt better or been in better shape in my whole life. This is nothing short of a miracle! I'm still astonished every day that this former fatty is living a "healthy lifestyle". This is a life I had given up on. I am here to tell you that if I can do it anyone can. I was obese, out of control, and definitely out of shape. I love telling people that I've lost 120 pounds. Their jaw drops with disbelief.

How did I make it through the holidays? It was easy. By this time I was so focused on showing-off my hard work, my new body. It was all about what I was going to wear. I wouldn't have cheated or binged on my diet if you paid me. I had worked hard and the big moment was about to arrive. Another way I was able to get through this weight loss process was I had a new sport…trying on clothes. At night when I was hungry and felt like eating and knew I had already consumed my calories for the day, I would go in my closet and try on clothes. As the months went on, this new hobby became more and more fun. It was a true source of motivation as I saw outfits begin to fit or become too big or actually even fall off. I highly recommend this activity when you feel like cheating.

-30 lbs. -50 lbs. -100 lbs.—and finally -120 lbs. Who would've "thunk" it? NOT ME! I want you to know that I never really thought I would be able to do it, yet somehow, with God's grace, the day arrived. I had lost the weight and it was time to go to the mart and win the bet. I was so nervous because I had envisioned this day for so long and it was finally here. I no longer sat in the chair feeling stuck—instead I could barely keep my feet on the ground.

What a moment! Everyone was surprised. Not only my betting colleague but all my friends and acquaintances I had met and worked beside at the mart over the years.

I felt like a celebrity. Everyone was so nice, so complimentary, and it was a very special day. The attention was overwhelming and made some of my shy characteristics come back to the surface. As I look back on that day, I can remember almost feeling embarrassed about my new body, as if I didn't deserve it or felt guilty for the way I looked. It had all happened so fast and I was not yet comfortable with my new look. I will never forget a friend who cheered me on through the whole tradeshow. He will never know how much his encouragement meant to me. As I continued exercising and time went by, this began to change. It took me a while to become comfortable in my new skin.

One of the biggest surprises to me from the weight loss was the reaction of my husband. I thought he would have been delighted. After all, he had wanted me to lose the weight for years. Instead of being excited, he began to not look at me and scarcely talked to me. At first I ignored it, but as time ticked by it became more and more obvious that something was wrong. By this time we had been married almost twenty-four years and I thought I knew everything about him. This was a new wrinkle in our relationship. At dinner one night I had to actually grab his face, make him look at me, and ask him what was wrong. It came down to the fact that he felt like his security blanket was gone. I couldn't believe it! While I certainly wanted to make him feel comfortable, I was not going to put on an almost 300 lb. fat suit again so he would feel secure. It has been a growing experience ever since. Be prepared for all kinds of changes in friendships and relationships.

I always tell my children there are some things in life that you can't change, such as how old you are, how tall you are, or the size of your feet. But there are plenty of things you can change. I had a thriving company and I was not at my healthy best. Just as I care about my business and how I package my product, it was time to care about myself and the package I present to my customers, family, and employees. What I learned from taking care of my own body spilled into every area of my life. My business has thrived because I have the self-confidence to stand up and present myself and my company the best way possible considering my age, my height and the size of my feet!

Finally, last but certainly not least, I could not have done the things needed to do for my company if I had not lost the weight and found myself again. My health and energy level continually amaze me. The energy you will need to develop and grow your business is astounding. Take your vitamins! Start an exercise routine—keep your spirits and body in tip-top health, because this is definitely an edge when it comes to staying in business.

Mentor Moment

Play hardball. Play for your life. You're better off for it now and later.

Chapter 7
MARKETING and PACKAGING

I love being creative and have appreciated all the mentors along my path. But then again, no woman is an island, right? It takes a smart and trusted team to be successful. Every day I am so thankful for those who have helped me every step of the way, those who popped-in and said just the right thing at the right time, and for my personal "barometer" to know what to do and when. It's my own sixth sense, my intuition and divine intervention that doesn't fail me. I may not always be right, but I love to learn and move on. I go to the school of hard-knocks but I try to make good grades. This is also a gift, I realize now.

Marketing and packaging is one of the most enjoyable, exciting, challenging and satisfying parts of any business. Without marketing and packaging you will have nothing more than a kitchen full of soap. There are a million ways to market and package your product or service. How you do this is key to your reputation, branding and the heart of your whole company. To set yourself apart from the rest of the marketplace, you should strive to be the most creative and innovative company out there. That allows you to compete with the best. You want to be cutting edge and ahead of the game.

You may have the talent to do this yourself or you may have to hire a person or a team of experts to get your product to market. As for myself, I could not afford to pay for outside help. Fortunately, I'm a fairly crafty-creative person and this comes easily to me. I also relied on all my friends and family for their advice and input; they were my test marketers. Yet in the end, you're the one with the vision and the final choice is yours.

As time went on, my product began to improve with small changes (better bags, classier ribbon, etc.). Don't rush. Think. Assess. Work through this process because your packaging will make or break your company. You may try an idea and it doesn't sell. It's not really a failure, just a less popular idea! With trial and error based on sound judgment you'll get it right. Don't be discouraged. Learn from each "non-sale" and listen to the advice of people around you. I still take a new prototype to trade shows and ask my customers, "What do you think of this?" They can be quite honest and you will get a feel if it will work or not. Once you have your initial packaging down and you feel sure that it's a winner, then it's time to market it—get it out there and sell your idea!

There are several levels on which to market your product or service. You can be strictly retail by placing it in your own store. You can sell retail at craft shows, especially to get started. I eventually chose to sell my product wholesale only. The profit margin is smaller but you can make up for it in volume. There are several ways to do this. You can use sales representatives (reps), sales groups, exhibit at trade shows or you can cold call customers.

Here's an example of creative, customized marketing: I decided to make a list of my top five dream-customers, the ones I'd always dreamt of supplying with my most magnificent products. All these companies were rock solid retailers to do business with and I thought and felt they "needed" my products. One in particular was focused on women and sold lotions, perfumes, and so forth, so we made up customized soaps that were pink and contained words like sexy, romance, angel, etc. We added delightfully pink/feminine/girly fragrances called "tickle me pink" and "pajama party" to name a few. I was living my dream and was beyond excited. We tied everything in the sheerest pink ribbons. The baskets of sample goodies looked and smelled fabulous. Now it was time to market it. I shipped the samples in perfectly presentable gift baskets nestled in boxes with a professional letter enclosed to what I thought was the correct buyer. Come to find out, I had sent them to the wrong person. Yet as it happened, the person who opened my sampler box was so excited that she called and gave me the name of the correct buyer. I told her to keep those for herself and I would reissue another box to the right buyer. I was grateful that this woman took the time to call me and give me the right person. A few days later I sent the soaps to the right buyer but heard nothing back. I called and called and when he finally called me back I wasn't there and missed his call. It took me four months to finally get an appointment to see him in New York.

At last! The day finally arrived to represent my company personally and fly to NYC to meet with the buyer of one of my top five dream clients. Their offices were on the 45th floor of the most gorgeous building, very historic with crystal chandeliers and posh everything. I've never seen views of NYC like that before, looking out their large windows. I met a man in the elevator whom I thought might be the man I was going to meet. I asked his name, nope not the buyer, but we ended up talking. He was there to see one of the buyers about buying his products. We ended up talking in the lobby and exchanged business cards. Always connecting and networking, I thought he might be useful one day and I loved his bottles.

The receptionist escorted me to the buyer's corner office with spectacular views of the Hudson River. I felt my heart racing. I had prepared for this visit—all my life actually—so I proudly, yet gently, began to lay out all my products. I gave it my best shot. He seemed less than interested. Keeping my spirits up, I could sense this detachment about the third second we met. He barely looked at what I was showing him. He was more interested in typing something on his computer than giving me a few minutes of his time. When I left not only was I disappointed, but I have to say I was even disgusted and felt disrespected. He'd made up his mind before I even showed up that he was not interested.

I wish I could say that all sales calls are successful, but they are not. It's best not to take it personally, yet when you place your heart into something as much as I have—and most likely you will—it's tough not to let it get you down. It was a big effort and expense to set all this up. Just don't allow yourself to wallow in self pity for more than a day, or half a day. You have more marketing and creating to do! I still believe that everything happens for a reason, and why I may not know for some time—until something good happens. I can often trace it back to being friendly, inquisitive and a hard-core student of the business world.

As it happens, I've now gotten a few quotes from the man that I met in the elevator. I am considering a new product using his products. So all in all, be prepared for many disappointments along the way, just don't let people like this get you down for very long. I'm sure at some point he will move on and I will still be here. I will not give up and I hope to get my chance there again. I know my product would do very well in their stores but he calls the shots now. I believe this and hopefully someday they will too.

I am now in three of the five stores on my wish list!

Mentor Moment
No need to thank me. You did it.

Chapter 8
BUSINESS BASICS
Attorneys, Insurance, Accounting—
the not-so-fun stuff for me

ATTORNEYS

If you are like most entrepreneurs, you are passionate about your product or service. This does not necessarily mean that you will like or want to deal with the not so fun stuff. By this I mean areas of business that are not your forte; they are your lesser strengths. That's life. Know yourself and then hire experts you can trust in your less passionate areas.

Personally, I don't like any of the organizational elements of setting up a business, but I need to do it anyway. I recall a friend told me early on that the first thing you need to do is hire a lawyer and an accountant. This is not what I wanted to hear, especially the lawyer part (no insult intended to my attorney buddies). This is excellent advice. If you are savvy with organizational structure, you may not need a lawyer at first. Yet at some point you will need counsel, whether it's to review a contract or to make sure you are staying in your legal limits. It's best not to wait until you're desperate. Ask other business people, especially those whose businesses are thriving. Do some research. Think for yourself and also surround yourself with wise people.

I had been in business for over two years when I finally spoke to an attorney. As I was picking his brains and he gave me some legal advice, he began asking some questions. One significant question was, "Do you have worker's compensation insurance?" I thought I did and stated that it was probably part of my insurance policy. He told me I had better check. I called the insurance company immediately and they said no, and I could not believe it. I had several employees by this time and could have really gotten myself in a bind had something happened. So while none of us wants to have to deal with injuries, health costs and the like, attorneys are a necessary part of being in business. I now have a great business attorney and even though he represents both my partner and me I am confident that he watches out for me first. You know you have a good attorney when they treat you as a friend.

Let's recap:

- Ask colleagues to recommend an attorney they know is fantastic and trustworthy
- Interview the attorney before a crisis occurs
- Come to an agreement that fits your budget (retainer or project based)

INSURANCE

You will need liability insurance! From day one you will need insurance. Don't risk your assets or personal possessions for your business. That automatically places everyone in a heightened stress zone. Initially, you may not need all that much coverage, but as your business grows so will your insurance needs. Invest in your company as it grows, so you are covered incrementally when your budget and income allow.

Shop around. Call, visit, and ask questions. Stay on top of it and interview different agencies. Ask their advice and keep files on each of several policy offers. Make sure you are being placed in the right category as this can greatly affect the price you will pay. Get at least three quotes before going with one. For instance, when I was getting quotes I was stunned at the premiums. When I began to question why it was so high we realized CFS as a company was not in the right insurance category. They had us as a chemical company instead of manufacturer and that one adjustment made a big difference in coverage and pricing. There are many kinds of insurance I have to carry: liability, property, inventory, and don't forget worker's compensation insurance. You don't have to have worker's comp insurance, as long as you are the only employee, but as soon as you hire your first employee this is a MUST!

- Find out for your category of business what types of insurance is recommended—a good insurance company will come to your place of business and do an audit to determine what you need.
- Shop around for the best quotes. Be careful and make sure you compare policy per policy the same coverage. (Compare apples to apples.)
- Never forget worker's compensation—a must have
- Increase your coverage as your business and inventory grows

ACCOUNTING

In the beginning of my business, I did the accounting myself (or at least attempted to) with the part-time help of a long-time family business accountant. A trusted accountant is an invaluable tool in any business, especially when getting started. One of the things that kept me going in my business was something that my accountant told me early on. I took her some soap samples and shared with her what I was doing. She said that she had been doing business accounting for twenty years and had seen a lot of businesses come and go—she thought this business was really going to make it. What a vote of confidence! Many times I've heard her words replayed in my mind when I was tired or discouraged. I appreciated and respected her opinion and believed what she said even when sometimes I lost heart myself.

Mentor Moment

• *Surround yourself with kind, peaceful, experienced experts who you know, know what they are doing.*

• *You don't have to know everything but you have to surround yourself with professionals who are experts you trust in their fields of expertise.*

You will need a Certified Public Accountant and financial advisor (CPA) for tax purposes. As you grow, at some point—unless you are brilliant with numbers—you will need an in-house part-time or full-time finance manager (bookkeeper plus accounting together in a position I call Chief Financial Officer, CFO). This is where I am super blessed. I am not an accounting whiz, nor do I particularly like keeping track of the finances. As a matter of fact, I have bounced more checks and paid more late fees than I care to think about. I could probably retire early from the monies I have wasted.

Nowadays I have a bookkeeper who is not only great at the financial stuff but actually likes it. Imagine that? Apologies to all of you who love this, but for me I can only be grateful to people who have skills I never could master. It takes all kinds to make the world go round and I am truly thankful for people who like to professionally play with numbers.

Mentor Moment
- Hire an accountant early on.
- Ask their business advice regularly—listen and implement it.
- Be on the lookout for an in-house financial person when the time comes to hire part-time and then full-time eventual employee.

CNBC's "The Big Idea" with Donny Deutsch
aired Nov 2007

Dawn and Michael (Paula Deen's husband)
Chicago 2007

One of Dawn's many appearances on QVC

Dawn and her original business mentor—her dad, Bill Green

Dawn and her sister Alison
at NY tradeshow

Dawn and Judy
"Best New Product"
NY Ex-Tracts Show 2006

Dawn and Sarah
(what a fat face)

Scoop Magazine Cover
July/August 2007

Dallaire Family
John, Sarah, Dawn, Sam

Photo from Atlanta
Journal Business Edition
January 2006

Larry, Dawn, Irv
Home & Housewares Show
Chicago 2007

First Tradeshow Booth — 2003

Tradeshow Booth
Americas' Mart Atlanta
2007

Georgia
COMMERCIAL
DRIVER'S LICENSE
EXPIRES 10-07-2006

SEX F
BIRTHDATE 10-07-1961
EXAM DATE 05-15-2002
COUNTY 056
HEIGHT 5-08
WEIGHT 185
CSC 01
FEE 008.00
RESTRICTIONS BV
CLASS B
ENDORSEMENTS P
TYPE CDL

OOPS
OFF BY 100LBS

BEFORE

Copy of Drivers License — 2002

Georgia
DRIVER'S LICENSE
EXPIRES 10-07-2016

SEX F
BIRTHDATE 10-07-1961
EXAM DATE 10-06-2006
COUNTY 056
HEIGHT 5-08
WEIGHT 145
CSC 87
FEE 035.00
RESTRICTIONS B
CLASS C
ENDORSEMENTS
TYPE REG
ORGAN DONOR

ONLY
OFF BY 20LBS

AFTER

Copy of Drivers License — 2006

Chapter 9
WHEN TO GROW, HOW TO GROW

HOW MUCH? HOW FAST?
One of the things my business mentor told me often was: **"Be careful not to grow yourself out of business."**

This made no sense to me for a long time. Why would you turn down business? Well, he was right. There are many ways you can grow yourself right out of a job. You can get yourself into real trouble, really fast, by having large debt, too much inventory, too many employees, and lag time between orders and payments from those orders, thus not being able to pay your bills. The whole scenario can come flooding in on you if you are not careful. This is something I still have to struggle with. However, having a business partner with a keen awareness of this helps keep me grounded.

Sometimes you just have to say, "No, thank you," and turn down business to take care of the business you have. You need to plan, pace yourself, plan again, and be careful not to take on more debt than you can handle. Taking on orders you can't ship because you lack finished products or enough employees can burn up your business, pronto.

Hiring the wrong staff (inefficient, incompetent people, etc.) when it seems like you need extra hands and not collecting your invoice money in a functional, timely manner are other critical issues. You can take a new loan and have that bank call-in your loan—yes, they can and they do. Options, when you have good credit you can use your equity line for potential business, then have that new client fall through. It happens. You can get into a habit of gambling right quick! I don't want to scare you, yet at the same time you should be forewarned and aware of some of the business pitfalls. I will say many times in this book, "Most businesses fail from lack of working capital." Know your limitations. Map out plans and revise them when you learn something new or bring in some extra cash.

EMPLOYEES

One day the hot water heater in my house broke and we called a plumber friend. As luck would have it, the hot water heater was in the garage where I was busy making soap. As we chatted, he became fascinated with the organized chaos that was taking place in my garage. Climbing over melting soap tubs was not his thing. Two weeks later he called and said his daughter needed a job and asked might I have anything she could do. I was just at the point where my home-grown business processes were becoming more than I could handle. I said, "Sure!" and with that, I had my first employee.

I was so excited because I knew the family and I sure needed help. Actually, I thought I had died and gone to heaven. She could tie ribbons on the soap bags as well, or even better than I could. Her working style proved peaceful and reliable. But would I be able to afford her long-term? Time would tell.

I once heard the leader of Costco say they always try and promote from within. I really like this concept because it's great for morale and it's often miraculous what people can do when given the opportunity. We now have twenty-three full-time and up to sixty-five part-time/temporary/seasonal employees on whom we rely. So keep your eyes and mind open for talent that's right in front of you. Give people a chance, especially from within your own business.

In our case, depending on how large an order we have, we often hire temporary workers. This can be done on your own or through a temp agency. The agency prices can vary greatly so shop around. There are pros and cons to each of these choices. The benefits of a temp agency are that they usually pay for the worker's comp insurance and taxes, which is costly to a beginner business. They usually offer health benefits that would be cost prohibitive as a temporary or smaller company employer. Your accountant will be better suited to help you decide if a temp agency or going it on your own and hiring part-timers is better. I've done both and feel that overall a temp agency is best. They do their homework and have screened their employees. While you will pay a fee for this workforce, it may be worth it for you as well. Also, if you are unhappy with a temp employee you just have to call the agency and let them know. They take care of this and you avoid the unpleasant task of have to fire someone.

For your full-time employees, you will have to decide if they are hourly or salary. Due to the buying cycle and seasonal purchase nature of my business most of our part-time or temp folks are hourly. I do have some salaried employees, but they did not start out that way.

I like trying people out first. This is another reason to hire partners or organizational people who are savvy in interviewing, hiring, and they can help you make these decisions. Besides experience in hiring, I find you have to be a people person. Anytime you work with folks, whether they are employees or customers, you have to be a team player, boosting and empowering all with whom you work. For some this comes naturally and for others it will have to be learned. It is almost the most important thing, though, that you realize colleagues on your team have to have good people skills to succeed in business. There are many self-help books out there to assist you with communication skills. And what would be your motivation? Making it or not. If you are shy and reserved, consider a partner. As my business partner says, "It's all about the relationships." When it's all said and done, in business and your personal life, it's all about win-win relationships.

Mentor Moment
Take the time to train people right. It will pay you back.

PARTNERS

Building relationships can lead to different and interesting avenues. It's important that all during your business life, you develop good, healthy and solid relationships for the long-term health of your business. You never know where these connections and friendships will take you. These relationships can include your vendors, customers or anyone else you encounter through your business. These could be your next investors, mentors, and business partners. Stay open and flexible, while paying attention to the work habits and styles of those path crossers you meet.

Staying open and learning from others happened to me in a big way. I developed a business relationship with one of my vendors, which grew into a trustworthy, professional friendship. This company and its team became my biggest ally. They helped guide me and kept me on track. I was able to ask them any questions because I knew they truly understood my business—and it was good for their business to help me. This was so important to the growth and prosperity of my company that we eventually grew into a very functional team. A lot of this book is based on advice and things learned from this great company and its leaders. It is always a good idea to surround yourself with people who have more expertise and training than you do in their particular field. It's not only good for your business; it's like getting a college education in real-world apprenticeships.

Mentor Moment

One thing my mother always told me was not to feel bad when you make a mistake—even if it costs you money. Chalk it up to college tuition. Learning is a lifelong process.

Don't be afraid to ask questions of other business people any time you can. For the most part, people like to share their stories and help—and you never know where a great connection will lead you. Not only did it greatly benefit me and my company, but in the end I was able to buy a lot more of this mentor's products and even move on to become business partners. It is a business relationship and friendship that was and is vital to my company and to me personally. After all, if your business is healthy, you feel healthier, too.

If or when you consider taking on a business partner there will be many things that you need to consider. It is best to do this when you are not frustrated or desperate. Sometimes these two things will push you, maybe even into making a rash decision. It is better to make a plan or proposal and sit on it, review it with trusted friends and family and do this when you are not under pressure. Business moves, business plans and reorganizations are, by definition, to be done with thought, care and for the good of the long-term wellness of your company. Here are some reasons to consider taking on a business partner or partners:

- Expansion, help with growth
- Financial, invest in the future of your company
- Share in decision making
- Offer expertise in areas that you don't have
- Marketing, combining business networks and relationships
- Help with increased workload

A partnership is very much like a marriage and if you do not want to have to divorce, you need to consider each partner carefully to see if this is a good match. This is why it's best if you're going to consider doing this not to do it when you are under pressure. For me, searching for a partner made sense. I was at a point when my business had grown to a level where I could no longer manage it alone. It was too much for me. No matter how many hours I put in, it was not enough. I could have just hired someone to help me; however, this partner came to the table with much more than that. He had an expertise in infrastructure, resources with decades of experience and expertise that I could not afford to simply hire.

The signs I mentioned above weighed heavily on me and thus forced me to realize what I knew deep down, that my company was ready to go to the next level, and I needed a team. This mentor relationship was the one to do it. CFS had grown way beyond anything that I had ever imagined. And it was precisely because I had built this relationship/friendship over several years that I knew I could trust this partner I was considering. There are a lot of articles on the web that will give you pros and cons in not only considering business partners, but mapping out a proposal and incorporating business planning into your decision. Do your research and make sure this is what you want. Partnerships are not for everyone. Take a course in business planning—three, five and even ten years out into your company's future. When the time comes you will be ready to make a sound decision based on some advice you acquired over a solid period of time and then took the time to mull over. It really comes down to personalities. We had compatible personalities along with mutual respect for each other. We had a solid friendship and I knew in my gut this was a good move on my part. This man had been the president of a multi-million dollar company and I was fortunate that he was willing to take a chance on my company. I value this partnership. I like having a co-decision maker. I rely on him often. Sometimes we don't always agree but we always have the best interest of the company and base our decisions on this.

Mentor Moment
It is most important to keep control, owning at least 51%. Do not give up control under any circumstances, even if you are desperate. If you do you will someday regret it.

If you choose the partnership route, you will want to have an outside legal advisor that you trust to help you define exactly what it is you want. It is important that you know your business goals and stick to them no matter what. Flexibility has its place, of course, yet you need to think about your goals as a business and personally; balance these goals and stick to them.

Before I made my partnership proposal, questions were swimming in my mind—some of which I am sure you have asked yourself: How much do you need to support your family? Do you have health insurance? Life insurance? Retirement, 401K? Think about what it is you really want and go for it. Some points in your life and your company's life will be non-negotiable and if you are forced to compromise on all of them then your proposed partnership is probably not the right partnership for you.

Once preliminary decisions are agreed upon and after you have negotiated a draft contract, you will have to hire an attorney to finalize it. Get help with this and do not try and do this on your own. It may cost you some monies up front but it can help keep you out of trouble down the road.

Mentor Moments

PARTNERSHIPS – Contract Negotiation TIPS
Here's to negotiating your way. It is a sample of an email conversation in which a merger is planned with a business associate. Preliminary ideas are shared and advice is given. Initially, I decided not to hire full-time, but in increments of time such as consultancy and project-based advice for pay.

- *KEEP 51% OF YOUR COMPANY NO MATTER WHO OFFERS WHAT.*
- *How often to have consultant time: Once a month for a full week.*
- *How to handle disagreements? You're the boss because you keep 51% no matter what. Your decision goes. However, listening, healthy communications and listing compromise possibilities will allow minds to work together for change and grow the business with each partner's opinions and advice.*
- *Partners' responsibilities will be what you want them to be. Create your own best business scenario. You know where you need assistance. You know your own talents. You stay in your talent zone. Delegate the rest. Define job roles of each partner and business team member. MAKE A BUSINESS PLAN TOGETHER AND FOLLOW IT; map out timelines and meet those timelines.*
- *You hire your people. You can use others' advice; however, you keep a handle on your staff and management teammates. You are the founder and main owner.*
- *You cannot stay in business unless you sell something. No matter what your talents, make sure your responsibilities oversee aggressive sales plans and designing, refining and/or enlarging or refining your product line.*
- *Define where you can do the most good and reap the highest sales with your focused time and effort expended. At some point, trade shows or business sales meetings can best be handled by trained reps or staff. Think long term and even how to train staff as a next step in expanding your business and delegating more to others. Save your energy for your favorite and most effective parts of your business for YOU.*

- Define together your partners' time commitment to you. Ask yourself: Are your merging partners spread too thin or focused exclusively on your company or somewhere in between? Make sure you do not put all your eggs in one partner's basket and that you have very clear job definitions, expectations and timeline goals to accomplish the work planned in your business plan.

- Be brave with your business plans. Make your dreams come true. Do not rely on any one exclusively—rely mainly on YOU. Create a professionally superior team that builds your company's reputation to the MAX. No person can do it alone, yet do not depend exclusively on any one partner.

- Don't sell-out to someone outside of your team. Talk over ideas. Chat about change. Do not spring something major on your team, especially your partners. Ask them first if you are even considering selling, or if a firm sent you an offer. Discussing this kind of large move with your current partners is essential for internal motivation and respect of each person in your management team. See everyone's point of view and make informed, well thought-out decisions. Growing, evolving and developing a stellar business is not a seat-of-your-pants, fly-by-night way of life and this haphazard thinking is not a viable solution to anything.

- Aim high with your expectations and goal for sales. Then create reasonable and practical steps and training to get where you want to be. For example, once you hit fifteen million in sales, you will be fine. Now walk backwards—what do you need to do to get there? Once your milestone is met, then set a next larger goal. Believing in your dream is a first step to getting there.

- Family members? Tread lightly on hiring them. Pretend they are not related and look exclusively at their qualifications and talents. My business mentor recommends you "Do Not" hire family members.
- Happiness Check: Anyone bored? Keep tabs on partners' creativity; allow it to flow for the development and exciting future of your business.
- When merging or partnering, give yourselves some time. A good rule of thumb is 3-5 years together before a large change in the original contractual agreement. This allows for market changes, slumps, rapid growth, illness, life changes, new products, and refinements of every business system and infrastructure you create as a unit, as a highly functioning team.
- Going public? Ask that question after meeting your business plan goals repeatedly. It may not be a best path for you. Investigate the process, keep open, collect information, but do not jump on this without great team agreement. Document your successes. File this in your corporate history. Keep track of your business sales trends. Going public requires loads of real numbers and track record data.
- Be nice to yourself. Plan vacation time. Stick to it. Keep your personal life in balance. Family + Business + Personal (health, wellness, time-out to replenish). The best life is a balanced one in which you actually perform better when you have time off and look at each sector of your life with fresh eyes.
- Have fun with new development that includes your partner or partners. You chose them for reasons. Enjoy the ride.

- *Know and own that you will make it. Believe it. See it every moment and in every choice. This is fundamental to dreams coming true and dreams do come true all the time. Look around. See the cup not only half full—see it overflowing!*

Chapter 10
PLAYING WITH THE "BIG BOYS"
Shopping Networks, Large Retailers, Wholesale Clubs, Barcodes, EDI Compliant, D&B & More...

Moving from individual and chain gift shops to playing with the "big boys" was my next business encounter. I listened to input, again, sometimes very opinionated input from my partner on this business focus. "Big boys" is an interesting term considering a lot of the buyers are women. Make no mistake about it; the playing field is very different with wholesale, larger quantity sales buyers. What an education I have received over these past years! In particular, no years have been as intense as the last two years as my company has ventured into this "grand" retail market. I appreciate the opportunity to share with you what I have learned so far and if it can help you in your business, then that makes this book worthwhile for me. I state "learned so far" because I am sure of one thing; there is a lifetime of learning yet to come.

First, you have to get your foot in the door, and this is no easy task. You will have to go back and rely on your persistence. I can't even begin to count the hundreds of unreturned messages and emails I have sent. Your skin will need to get tough. I've been rejected more times than I want to remember and this is hard because like many sensitive people, I take things personally. By this "big boy" client time, you will have invested your life's blood into your business and you can't help being affected by "no's". Don't feel rejected—focus on your niche and where you best fit in, that's all. If you still believe in your product and you know it sells if only you are given the chance then NEVER GIVE UP!!!! As my mentor has always told me, "If you keep trying, something will eventually hit."

For example, a major retailer in the bath industry would not give me the time of day two years ago, yet I'm writing this sitting on a plane headed to their competitor's corporate offices to make a presentation. So if one door closes go right ahead and knock on the other. You can get your foot in the door by calling the corporate offices and getting the correct name of the buyers. Sometimes this works. Often, or usually, the buyers do not answer and rarely return phone calls. Try email and re-emailing. If you can get their specific, regularly answered email, I suggest sending gorgeous photos promoting your product or service.

Another choice is to hire part-time sales-reps, or what I have found works, brokers. Brokers are a form of sales-reps but their commissions are not so high, usually around 5%, and they only deal with the larger retailers. (I love saying that I am a "larger retailer" now!) The sales reps I use I personally met at trade shows. One even saw an article on my business in the local paper and stopped by my trade show booth. These reps already have relationships established with the buyers.

A favorite product term buyers are interested in is "sell throughs". They want to know how much of your merchandise they can "sell through" in the short amount of time. They like to see upwards of 70% sell-throughs within a few weeks. That's turn around, like a restaurant that calculates how many times they need to "turn around" a table to make a profit in any one day. This is the same thing in any sales-oriented business. Document your sales. Graph the results client per client. Once you have some sell-through numbers from one company then you will be able to predict or forecast to your new potential customers the sell-throughs that you've experienced with other large retailers. Different retailers request or require different kinds of margins. For instance the larger retailer and shopping network retailers like to make about 40 - 50% margins, whereas a warehouse retailer such as Costco or Sam's Club only needs 15% margins. Margins are different than mark-up percents.

Mentor Moment
   Be willing to give mark down monies if your product doesn't sell.

The warehouse retailers will usually want your product in sets or kits rather than selling individually. Be ready to "sharpen your pencils" as they will say and offer a special-only-to-them exclusive kit or package deal. Warehouse volumes will usually compensate for any price reductions you will have to make to get your *set* on their shelves. Before you can "sharpen your pencils", you will need to interview or ask them what kind of quantities they are talking about and the estimated ship date they will need.

QUESTIONS TO ASK LARGER RETAIL BUYERS:
- What quantities are you talking about?
- Who pays for shipping?
- When do you need it?

- Are there mark-down monies?
- What are the hidden charges? (Advertising etc.)
- Is this done through EDI?
- What are the terms?
- What price are you paying for your merchandise?
- How do you want it boxed?

Many times they will even ask you not to sell the same program to their competitor. This is why I mentioned above offering them an "exclusive" kit or set of your products. You must assess all of this. If their order is large enough and you can see real potential then I usually agree to fully customize the items. If the order is not, then I would not agree. This is a decision you will have to make for your company when the time comes, on a per customer basis. It depends also on your employee pool and other logistics of your organization. As I have said before, don't commit to something you can't do and whatever you do, do not order product without a purchase order in hand or you risk getting stuck with an "almost" order and a small company cannot often take a hit like this.

Mentor Moment

(again, yes, again) "MOST businesses fail from lack of working capital."

When clients buy in quantity then you can buy your supplies in quantity and also lower your cost. By the time you are at the point to start dealing with the larger retailers you should already know the bulk rates of your next level of purchase, especially from your top vendors.

This is a perfect time to have good, sound financial advisors. This is where a good bookkeeper/comptroller is essential. They will keep you out of trouble and from getting over your head.

Most, if not all, large volume retailers will want you to be "EDI Compliant". What is EDI compliant? Well, I will try to explain it in the best and simplest way I can. To start with, EDI stands for "Electronic Data Integration." It's a way of making your life miserable. Just kidding—well sort of. There are many charge backs if you do not get it right. Each item, case, inner carton and outer carton will have to have barcodes. Each bar code is applied in a specific location and there is information linked to each bar code. It can be quite intimidating. It is a process that in the early part of my business I attempted to become EDI compliant. I was not ready for this and I failed miserably. My business was not large enough and I did not have the right team for this. It was a disaster. This experience also made me gun-shy. However, I knew if my company was going to move to the next level it was essential. There are companies that will help you and you can do this online. When a retailer requires this of you they will also recommend an outside source to help you with it. It's not my favorite thing to do even now, but it's better with the right help. Do not attempt to be EDI compliant alone. Do your research and ask for help.

Mentor Moment
Many successful businesses start from passion. The way to compete with the "big boys" is to have a breakthrough product, be smarter, faster, and more efficient and have funds to accomplish what you want.

Chapter 11
TRADESHOWS

At some point you will probably want to exhibit at a tradeshow related to your industry. This is one of the most effective tools to promote your product or service. I have been doing tradeshows since I started, which seems like a lifetime ago. You will quickly go from the very inexperienced new kid on the block to "senior exhibitor", because the shows are so intense and you are *on*, you are going 100 miles a minute on your feet speaking about your products for hours and hours. Tradeshows can be a lot of fun even though they are physically and mentally demanding because you develop relationships that can make or break your business.

The best thing for me, I've found, is to prep myself for the shows, so I am at my best. This means going to the gym every day before and after the show and if I am at an accommodating hotel, I try to go to the gym during the show days—even though my mind doesn't want to work-out after twelve-hour tradeshow days. I am at my happiest and best if I keep to my eating right and exercise routine. I also make sure my nails and hair are done and my wardrobe is in order. The older I get the more work it takes.

As with anything in life, you get out what you put into it. Tradeshows are definitely the way to go—and for a company without a retail showroom, tradeshows are your commercial reputation and your window dressing for the world. I am still amazed at the lack of planning and poor display booths I see at shows. And then other exhibitors wonder why they're not busy. A wrinkled tablecloth on a cheap table does not cut it. Tradeshows cost tens of thousands of dollars to orchestrate, and the last thing you want to do is skimp on showcasing your product. Make sure you display your product at its best. My advice is to research which shows host your kind of product, see what displays have been showcased in past shows, and spend some good advertising dollars toward an up-to-date showcase for your products.

Which tradeshows to attend? Internet research your product field, search-out a few shows and obtain some contact names with telephone numbers. Then ask others, so you can best the best at the shows you choose to attend. Here are some key questions to ask of the people putting on the tradeshow:

- How many buyers attended the last show?
- Would you send me a map of the next tradeshow floor and which booths are available?
- Where are my competitors located?

How to use this information is key. It's all about LOCATION, LOCATION, LOCATION. Each time I do a new show I call and ask which available space is the best location. I always tell the show manager that I'm relying on them and to please give me the best location possible to showcase my fun soaps. I prefer a corner booth, even though it costs a little more. Lighting is also important. You can either buy your own lighting or rent it from the show services. Spotlighting your products makes everything sparkle and shine—it really does make a difference to seasoned buyers, especially those "big boys" that I've mentioned earlier.

Do your homework when it comes to doing your first tradeshow. Use the excitement and fear to your advantage—talk with passion, have a love for your product line, so you can literally talk-through your apprehension about anything. This creates a fun attitude toward your future business and can carry you through the tons of paperwork you will have to fill out, and the hours of stamina you'll have to muster. It is important that you get your paperwork and order forms in on time. This will save you a lot of money; take advantage and register for early bird rates. Organizers always have deadlines to order your tables, electricity, etc. If you miss your deadline the price goes up.

If you have lingering questions before the show, by all means CALL the personnel who are putting on the tradeshow; don't go without answers. They are used to dealing with first-time exhibitors and are there to help you be successful, which makes them successful as events planners. Again, keep researching. Know the going rates. Plan how many shows you can afford to attend each year and plan for some fun. Be informed. Ask away! There can be a lot of hidden charges, plus, each show is run differently. You will soon learn how they work after attending some.

In preparation for my first tradeshow booth design, we taped out a 10' x 10' on my living room floor. I began to play with the space and how I wanted the traffic flow to work. This lets you know how much space you have to work with. You can completely set up your booth and then pack it right from your set-up space. This will help assure that you've not left anything out. You can research tradeshow booths online. The ones I found online were usually expensive for highest-end tradeshow displays. (See the center photo section, where there are pictures of some of my booths, even my very first one.) You don't have to spend a lot of money to be effective, but you only have one first-impression on a buyer to get them to glance your way and draw them in. Even though my first booth was a little "hokey and homemade" looking, it was clean, colorful and fun to visit. I still do a lot of the same things today that I did when I started out. I was afraid to begin with one of the larger shows like Atlanta or New York. I opted for a medium size show in Orlando. This was probably a good decision at that time since I was doing everything myself. However, once you are comfortable that you can deliver what you sell, then stretch yourself and your business and do some larger shows. They give you better exposure, larger buyers and it's not that much more work to do the larger shows than it is to do the smaller ones.

A first step to help you ease into this arena is to go and walk a tradeshow before you set up for an exhibit. I did not do this since I was late signing up, it was in another state, and I just couldn't swing two trips. If my memory serves me correctly, I think my first trade show including hotel, food and travel expenses, was about $2300. I took orders for a little more than $5000. I have to say I was a little disappointed; I had imagined selling much more. I really had no idea what to expect and, in hindsight, that wasn't so bad. My product was far from perfect and my line was limited. Don't expect to make millions at these shows. It takes time to build your customer base and get your product known. You have to follow-up. Rome wasn't built in a day. Don't be discouraged if your first venture is less than spectacular.

A practical goal for attending a tradeshow? Break-even and have fun meeting colleagues. Learn from it! Talk to everyone around you. Find out what tradeshows they like, ask questions, make friends. And learn to "close the deal" with every potential client you meet! Ask every potential buyer for their business card. Keep them by your phone for follow-ups.

I have met so many good friends over the years from these shows. One of my favorites is Judith Beard from "Lucky Me." She and I met at a tiny trade show in Panama City Beach, Florida. It was my second tradeshow and her first and we were so green, we laughed at everything and found we had much in common. And to this day, we still share commonalities, as both of our businesses have grown leaps and bounds and we go to even more shows now. We often see one another at tradeshows all over the country and still have the best time together. We went to New York this year to a show where only magazine editors attended; we shared a room to save on expenses. What a good time we had!

Another tradeshow friend, Robert Hernandez, of the "Seda France" candle company, is so talented with the most beautiful booths—bar none. Every morning before the shows, I would find his booth and just stare, drinking-in his creativity. He's won "Best Booth" from coast to coast. I am constantly amazed every time I see him. And to think our friendship started because I admired his booth so much, I wouldn't go away! We recently shared a fabulous dinner during the San Francisco Gift Fair. He has given me great business advice over the years, to be sure. So, be friendly and learn when you go to these shows. We are all in this together trying to make a living.

A last tip for the weary: be flexible and patient when you are setting up and breaking down your booth. The tradeshow union can be frustrating and most always something goes wrong, so expect it and CHILL. I am an impatient person and I hate breaking down and waiting for help packing everything in my crate. My business partner tells me that my real talent lies not in soap making but in "crate finding". I've been known to go down freight elevators with union workers, climbing over others' crates to find mine. I've even used bribery (not recommended) a few times. It is a bit of a gypsy life that can be a lot of fun, too.

Mentor Moment

Below are some terms and definitions that you will need to know and ask as you enter the world of tradeshows:

Crate – you will be charged for over-sized and over-weight crates. You can caravan your crate from one show to the next for a lower cost than shipping it directly yourself.

Booth space – what is the average—what can you afford—are there any obstructions in your booth—what are the walls made of—what's on the floor—what can you afford?

Deadlines – watch your deadlines for crate shipment, electricity, lights, tables, chairs, etc. This will save you money!!

POV – *privately owned vehicle. There is usually a charge for delivering your products in your own vehicle.*

Temporaries – *booths that are set up on a temporary basis for the show.*

Permanents – *those who are in permanent showrooms.*

Standard Booth Equipment – *this is complimentary and usually includes a table, chairs and a wastebasket. However, you still have to put your order in for this by the deadline or it will cost you once you arrive*

Drayage – *material handling*

TIPS TO MAXIMIZE YOUR BOOTH EXPOSURE

• Feature your best, most exciting products prominently.

• Ask buyers feedback on what's selling in their stores.

• Make sure your booth is adequately staffed. The busiest hours are from 11A.M. – 3P.M.

• Discourage your staff from eating, sitting and drinking while in the booth. Buyers tend to pass the booths that look like they are closed for lunch.

• Wear clothing that projects the image you want.

• Have pre-printed order forms to expedite the order process.

• Staple customers' business card to your copy of the order form.

• Be professional and courteous. Treat your customer with respect and they'll keep coming back.

• Don't talk on your cell phone during show hours.

Chapter 12
FINANCING YOUR BUSINESS

I was on my third week of aggressively searching for a bank to lend me money for Clearly Fun Soap. Every morning I would wake up and put on my business best. It was summer in the south and this was no fun task. It was hot and I was literally hitting the pavement. I kept in mind stories of people getting turned down many times (even Coca-Cola had tons of "no's" before someone took a chance on their formula!) as I headed off each day trying not to get my feelings hurt. I called ahead, made appointments, and even sometimes dropped by unannounced. This is not such a good idea as busy banks can leave you waiting for a long time.

I brought along all of my key paperwork and filled out countless financial applications, pleading my story day after day, bank after bank. Toward the end of this money-finding period, I found myself getting hostile and cynical, which is out of character for me. I resented that I was spreading my personal and business information all over town with people I didn't know looking at it. I had to remind myself often why I was doing this and kicked myself for not doing it earlier as I had been told many times by my mentor.

I needed money and I was in dire straights, needing financing quickly with some large orders pending. In actuality, however, this really motivated me to get going in spite of the heat. Financing your business can be the biggest challenge you will face. There are many ways to go about it.

Most successful businesses at some point will need financing to grow. **Again, a number one reason that businesses fail is lack of working capital.** This advice was given to me early on in my career and I never forgot it. You will hear this several times in the book. Make no mistake. I repeat this because it is so important.

I tried postponing loan financing as long as possible because I didn't want to get over my head. Yet the day came when I needed more working capital to keep up with the demand—essentially a good thing. I almost waited too late and it put a real strain on me financially, as well as emotionally.

There are many options to finance, but there are some requirements that almost all of them will want from you. Again, I cannot stress enough how important it is to have a game plan.

Mentor Moment

Business Topics to Resolve and Documents to have ready for Financial Applications and Loan Interviews:

- *Business plan – You can research online how to do this. The SBA website gives you business plan guidelines; create and 1-2 times yearly revise your company's plan.*
- *Personal Financial Statement – This form can be obtained at most any bank.*
- *Your last two years corporate returns*
- *Your last two years personal returns*
- *Accounts Receivables*
- *Purchase Orders*
- *Inventory, if available*

Obtaining a loan can be one of the most frustrating challenges you will face. It literally took me over a year to secure my first major business-building loan. I have often wondered if it is an area in which women are still discriminated against. As time has gone on, I think perhaps being a woman can also work to an advantage. There are loans that are specifically designed for women in business. They are hard to obtain and can take a lot of time and work. If you have the time, then you may want to explore this. Unfortunately, I was in a time-crunch and this was not an option for CFS. I will never know if it would have been easier if I had been a man, but I can't help but wonder. Regardless, it can be done.

I like the idea of supporting a local bank and building a reputation in your hometown. I know banks have strict regulations but they still have some flexibility. I quickly learned, whether you are a local business or not, banks require collateral, especially in the form of real estate and not purchase orders. I went to nine banks before I finally got two of them to take me seriously.

I could not understand how I could go to a bank, after being in business for over three years with a lot of good sized purchase orders in hand, and not be able to obtain a loan for only 10% of the orders. The orders were from a reputable company with a proven track record of paying their bills. And for me there would be little risk for a bank and I knew I was right. I kept on keeping on! I did not think this was an unreasonable request, but you would have thought it was like asking for a million dollars by the way they reacted: no, no and more "no's"!

> ### Mentor Moment
> *It's in the attitude. You are going to have to learn to go over your head a bit. Most businesses cannot operate without borrowing. You'll have to stay ahead of the money game and you will be just fine—that means pay your bills on time. Collect your receivables. Our company has been working with bank loans for years. It can cause stress if you take it that way; growth involves a little stress and a few loans. Change your mindset and get creative about financing your development!*

Almost every bank referred me to a factoring company, which is a company that will loan you money against your receivables. However, your customers will send the checks to the factoring company and not to you. There are also fees and high interest to pay for this type of loan. One bank even brought their factoring representative with them before they knew anything about me. I was fortunate that I had a banking mentor, a longtime friend who had already given me a heads-up on what factoring was about. He gave me a list of questions to ask. I personally feel that factoring should only be used as a last solution. Had I not been able to finally obtain a loan, I may have been forced to do this. It is something I did not feel comfortable doing. You can do more research on the Internet to see if factoring will work for you. Again, I would only use this as a last resort. They generally loan you up to 80% of your accounts receivables and not on your purchase orders. They then take over your accounts receivable and collect the money themselves. Be careful if you go this route and do your homework. Know what you are getting into.

There are also companies who will loan you money on your purchase orders but the interest rate is generally high and they also take over your monies. Watch for hidden charges and fees. It's always best to obtain an SBA (Small Business Administration) loan or a line of credit. There are also some fees related to the SBA loan but these are the best loans, in my opinion. These are some questions you will want to ask when choosing a bank for a loan or equity line of credit:

- What are the closing costs?
- When are the payments due?
- What is prime (right now, it changes)?
- How many points over prime?
- Is this a line of credit or terms?
- Is there a penalty for paying it off early?

Don't give up. Be persistent. Remember, I was turned down by seven banks before I finally found two that were willing to take a chance on CFS and me. It is hard work and often frustrating, but it will pay off when the time is right for your business to expand. If you can get more than one bank to loan you the money, always choose the best deal for your company. You will know this by asking the above questions and comparing banks.

About the time I had just about exhausted every bank in town a couple of bankers came by my office. I felt incredibly frustrated and told these two men if they weren't going to help me now, when I needed help, then when? Trying to stay with local banks, I told them in a few weeks when I secured a loan they didn't have to even think to come anywhere near me and try to get my business in the future. My money was going with whoever was willing to help me now. I said this with force and conviction. I think I scared them a little. I can't even remember now if this was the bank that eventually loaned me the money. But I can promise you that when I got paid that my money stayed with the local bank that was willing to take a chance on me. They have turned out to be a great ally and they are definitely glad they took the risk.

After the large order was completed and we had been paid, the local lending bank called and it scared me because usually when a bank called me in the past, it was because I messed up something or had bounced more checks. My heart was pounding and the voice on the other end asked me if there was anything they could do for me and if I'd like them to raise my line of credit! I tried not to let them know I almost fell off the chair. I breathed in to calm my excitement and told them that would be great. They didn't know I didn't need it right then but the one lesson I've learned is to get lines of credit while you can!

Several months later, the *Atlanta Journal Constitution* newspaper ran a big article on CFS and my story. The day it came out, as soon as I arrived to work, the phone rang. It was a banker and he said he just happened to be in the area, read my article and would like to stop by. I said, "Sure". Boy, he gave me his best pitch. But my still-raw emotions from searching and searching for loans came back to the surface and I reminded him that his bank had originally turned me down. He was sure it wasn't him since he was new to this bank and named his previous bank employer. I again told him that bank had turned me down also. I had no intention whatsoever of changing banks and he soon realized this and humbly left. While I felt a little bad for him, I was giggling a little under my breath, as well. People are drawn to success and I was finally being viewed as successful and it felt wonderful. Plus, I'm loyal to those who help me.

Later in my career, when I decided to grow more and invite a partner in, something that totally amazed me after I took on my business partner was his approach to financing. From day one of our new agreements, he was on the offense, readying and aggressive to get more working capital. He already knew his strategy before arriving at my headquarters. In the first week he met my local hometown banking team and set up meetings with a larger bank to start building relationships for the future. I was totally fascinated. Why hadn't I done that earlier? What stopped me? I had always been passionate about my business. And, at this phase of our partnership, we certainly didn't need the financing. Thinking ahead, though, he shared our business plan and how our business operates, and left it that if the right order were to come through we would need them, and quickly. He had them eating out of his hand. I love this—and I didn't have to be the only one asking! This is where surrounding yourself with people who have talent in your lesser strengths can be an asset and helps you plan for expansion for the future. It is a vital attitude for the long-term sustainability of your company.

A lot of people are afraid of money. I have come to realize that money is a friend and it greases the wheel of success. As my mentor has said before, "The number one reason businesses go under is from lack of working capital." So, as you can see, having a line of credit ahead of time is instrumental in planning for your lifelong success. Set yourself up now for success.

Mentor Moment:

- *Don't give your power away.*
- *Credit report services or listings in Dun and Bradstreet have their reputations. These services do collect information FREE and then charge others for it. Think. Assess for yourself. Ask your teammates and trust friends. You can neither guarantee nor buy success. Obtain information about companies you wish to market and sell to, but stop at sending your financials around. When you need credit, yes, selectively place your valuable information to only your clients or potential lenders.*

Chapter 13
EGGS IN A BASKET
Building Your Client Customer Base

As your business and customer base grows, and your name and product begin to infiltrate the marketplace, don't be surprised if you get interest from larger accounts. While this will be great news, there are several things you need know, from my point-of-view. First of all do not promise what you can't deliver or that will be your first and only chance as a potential supplier. These buyers expect you to do what you say and in the timeframe you've agreed upon. It's better to be honest than to get caught not being able to fill your order on time. However, if it is at all possible you must go for it—even if it pushes you to the limit, along with everyone around you. Good business takes calculated risks.

I remember one of my first large orders came in for frog soaps. At this time we were working out of my house. We had frog soaps on every available surface! My dining room table was a sea of frogs. When it came time to load the boxes on pallets we had no loading dock so we made a line of family and friends and we loaded boxes onto a pallet in the back of my husband's pick-up truck. We then ran it up to my uncle's business, unloaded it and did it all over again. The day we were loading the truck with boxes I saw someone in my house take a hand truck and scrape it across my hardwood floors to load a stack of boxes. I knew then and there that this was moving out of my house! If I did not, my house would have eventually been ruined.

You don't want to miss an opportunity. Just please know that if you are willing to do whatever it takes to fulfill your obligation, you guarantee your own success. Treat that large purchase order as a signed contract, because in many ways it is! Contracts come complete with deadlines. You can literally ruin your company's reputation by not making your deadline, plus you could be out a lot of money. If you are not too far off the deadline, perhaps some companies may be willing to give you a little grace, but make sure by communicating with them as your order comes along, even if you are running late!

Another thing to keep in mind is not to grow too fast. You can grow yourself out of business by growing too fast. By the time these opportunities present themselves you will have a lot of experience under your belt and should be able to make these decisions. While I don't want to scare you, keep these cautions in the back of your mind. Another trap you don't want to fall into, even though it's very hard not to do, is "keeping your eggs all in one basket." It will be good while it's good but be prepared, especially if you are in the retail market. It changes fast and you can be cut loose without warning. This has happened to me and I must warn you to keep your business strong. It is better to have twenty $100,000 dollar accounts than one $2,000,000 dollar account. This way if one or two fall by the wayside your company is still strong.

Mentor Moment

- *Keep an open dialogue with your buyers.*
- *Don't put all your company's future into one or two customers' baskets. Build your client base. Respect their orders. Deliver them. Follow-up, asking for feedback. Listen and act on that feedback, thus diving right back into that all important relationship building.*

Chapter 14
BALANCING PERSONAL and PROFESSIONAL LIFE

Can you have it all? Yes, no, and maybe.

There are some days when it seems as if I can have it all, but there are many days when the answer will be no. The answer is most likely a maybe at best.

What does having it all really mean? I have a business and a personal life, and to be honest that's enough. I don't want it all. Sure, I do want to be successful at what I have. The balance between business and personal is many times a difficult one. I guess that's putting it mildly, that said from my motherhood-hat viewpoint.

What it boils down to, for me, is that life is about being happy and grateful for what you have right in front of you, right now, right here. Can I smile, even feel warm all over for what is on this day's plate? You bet I can. So consider that if you are grateful for what you are doing and who you are while you are doing it, perhaps that is the best personalized definition "having it all" can mean for any one of us.

An attitude of gratitude—that's what I say. It's your attitude and the color of the glasses you wear, as you look out onto your life, that matters immensely. By nature, I am a happy person. I was going through a difficult time and a good friend of mine said, "You are a happy-miserable person!" That about says it—that's me. No matter what I go through, I believe a good attitude can only help and for me it gets me moving out of the dumps and motivates me to see the next light around the bend.

And life has changed considerably. Back when I began *Clearly Fun Soap*, my intention was to continue staying at home, "momming" with some work on the side. I never in my wildest dreams imagined what would happen, has happened and is planned to happen in my life now. I am grateful beyond measure that I didn't start this until my son and daughter were both off to school. I started when my youngest child, Sarah, went to kindergarten. I am so glad that I was able to stay home with them during those early years, because that was important to me and for them in those formative years.

Funny. They don't actually remember much about this time, when I was home, nurturing them full-time. They think I work all the time and travel a lot. For me, in our society and in the culture I was raised, being a working mom is one of the hardest things I've ever had to deal with emotionally. It's very hard when you are out of town and your child calls you needing something. Is this having it all? The love of your children, yet you can't hug them *right now*. I can't answer that for you; it seems my answer changes for me, given any certain day or city in which I find myself.

These are just a few of the difficult things I've had to deal with and I am sure either as a parent yourself or in life with children somewhere in the mix, you know the struggles, too. It's during these times that I remind myself why I'm doing this and why IT IS worth it. First off, we need to eat and have a place to sleep. I did not necessarily want it to be like it is, but then again, I don't believe we have the control over our lives that we think we have. Sometimes life takes us on a path that is not always pleasant, to get us to where we are supposed to be. I never imagined when I was a little girl that I'd grow up and own a soap business, or any business for that matter. And at the same time, I do believe God has this plan for me and this is where I have ended up.

After all, I came from a family of entrepreneurs and I was at a place where I had to make my own way or we would be in serious financial trouble. Plus, I also want to be an example to my children, a model for creativity and excitement for life, which is certainly how I feel most days when I do head off to work. I wish it were simple, but it is not. We all have choices that maybe our own parents did not have: you can stay at home, work outside the home, maybe both. Whatever you choose, the bills still have to be paid. You can always buy a smaller house or even rent to keep your bills down, but you still have to pay the bills. As I've quoted more than once, "Everything comes at a price, even doing nothing." I have had my share of jobs I didn't like. So as hard as it can be to balance personal and business life, at least I love this job. I get to be an inventor, a customizer, a creative person, and learn things I never even knew existed. Every day is chock-full of opportunity. I feel this is a gift for my family and me. Don't you?

As my children grew and matured, they have actually begun to appreciate and respect the fact that I have to work. They've also seen the rewards of having a happy mother and, upon occasion, they enjoy participating in the creative process. For example, in the summer of 2007, Sarah, my ten year old, came to work with Mommy. She took a piece of paper and titled it "my new idea." She sketched and colored a bath set full of soap goodies in a clear box with a cardboard bottom. She listed the dimensions and the price she thought it should retail for. This was a proud moment for me.

What do I have to feel guilty about?

Why am I worrying?

Aren't we all the best parents we can be, given our circumstances?

Aren't we—man or woman—just trying to be the best we can be and get along, perhaps get along really well?

I will choose not to worry so much and keep my mental state healthy. I strive to be successful in both my business and family life. Life holds no guarantees. I do not know if I am doing it right or wrong but I am doing it, and to the best of my ability. And if I do not know something, I am willing to investigate, research and educate myself in doing it better. Only time will tell. So far we have managed to eat well, keep a beautiful roof over our head and even take a vacation here and there.

There are times when I start that pit-in-my-gut guilty feeling, but we are fortunate that we live in a day in which cell phones and emails allow us to be accessible for our family members 24/7. And when I am home I make sure there are lots of hugs and attention given. Someone recently told me that:

Listening is loving.

I try and sit with each of my kids and my husband and genuinely listen—give them quality *me* time. I really can't say what is best for you. It's a societal struggle that may never be resolved—family balance is a continual issue for most. I am still working this out daily and I'm sure, even when my children are grown, it will be a lifelong process balancing all the hats I wear—and wear happily.

Chapter 15
BENEFITS OF BEING A WOMAN IN BUSINESS

The trials and triumphs of being a woman in business in a man's world is a main issue on why I wanted to write this book. As you have seen, the trials and triumphs have been many and **I AM** a woman in business in a man's world—whether I am a successful one is still up in the air. However, it is no longer, nor will it ever be again, solely a man's world. Women have infused the business world decades ago and continue to do so at a rapid pace. Gone are the days when men were the primary business owners. I think that men, for the most part, have embraced the idea that women are, and even think deep down that we can be, good at business. Gone are the days when women were the ones in the kitchen. Some of the greatest chefs now are men. Some of the greatest business owners are now and will be women. We have a lot to offer the business world, just as male chefs have a lot to offer the culinary world.

Whether it is by necessity or choice that you become a successful business owner, **YOU CAN** make a difference in the world. I believe that the benefits of being a woman in business far outweigh the disadvantages. I feel strongly that women are a wonderful complement for our male counterparts. And for the most part, men like working and dealing with women. We may or may not have been taught business basics from an early age, but we can become quick studies. Some are like me and have always been surrounded by entrepreneurs such as my parents and family members. I have learned by their example. It's important to soak in what is around you. Be flexible and be open minded, learn, assess what's right for you, and then listen some more!

We can also be a fantastic example to our children and break some of those stereotypes to which we've all been exposed. We can offer the business world our color, our creativity, our compassion, and uniquely different perspectives. While I love being a woman in business, I also love being a woman. I never want to lose the benefits of being a woman. It's important to be true to yourself. You can be feminine and strong. You can have compassion and still maintain control of your company.

People attract people. Call it chemistry, fate or the law of attraction. Use it, pick peoples' brains, take men or women out to dinner—do whatever it takes to learn from all of these "path crossers" in your life. I am an insatiable learner and I want to know what makes people successful. Business stories fascinate me! After all, there are over 6 billion people in the world. Why are they here, if not to build relationships? Start developing your business network now. Make friends with those you connect with or have chemistry with. Don't let any opportunity to learn and grow pass you by. Use common interests and attraction, whether with men or women, to build lifelong relationships.

Mentor Moment TIPS:

- *Google women in business. Learn about any programs to boost women in business. They are out there. Think globally.*

- *Find your personal drive and use your instincts. Never underestimate a woman's intuition. Go with your gut. Listen to your inner self. Stay true to who you are and what you stand for. This keeps you mentally healthy and alert.*

- *Find someone to share your true business feelings with, don't keep them bottled up inside. It can be a trusted business mentor or family friend but you need someone to share your business trials and triumphs. It fuels your creativity, helps shoulder the load. It's no fun to go it alone.*

- *Beware of jealousy and nay sayers. Stay away from the "Border Bullies," as I call them. These are the folks who stand on the edge of your dreams and tell you why you can't have them. (The term "Border Bullies" comes from the wonderful book, "The Dream Giver", by Bruce Wilkinson.) There are also spiritual vultures, who are out to give you the opposite side of your upbeat positive self. Learn quickly who genuinely cares for you and your business.*

- *Be aware of crooks.*

Very early on one of my vendors became intrigued with Clearly Fun. He has helped guide me through the many daily challenges a business encounters. Through all of this a great and beneficial friendship emerged. I could not, nor would I want to, have experienced all of this without him. When good things (and bad) happened in my business I could hardly wait to share the news with him. His decades-long expertise and experience in an industry related to mine not only greatly benefited my business, but in turn, I benefited his company also. His wise advice and counsel have proven invaluable to my business.

Sometimes experienced or expert mentors are family members, and sometimes not. I have loved the fact that I know my dad, my original business roll model, is proud of my success.

And last but not least, my husband, who has been very supportive from day one.

When you start a new business or invent something new you should always remember: "We stand on the shoulders of giants," Jonas Salk, inventor of penicillin stated. We're always improving on our ancestors' work and honestly, we don't do anything alone. It's not so much about the destination but the ride to get there! Find as many trusted people as you can to share your ride. And, have fun!

The fact that I have lost a lot of weight and have a successful business has posed many interesting twists and challenges. I have seen friends and even family members struggle with "the new me" and adjusting to the new me. Some odd behaviors took me by surprise. People do not like change and wish everything—including me—could stay the same. They like for you to stay in the box *they've created for you*. Once you emerge from your old box (your old self), sometimes people can't get "the old you" they know—and they try to put you back into their box! Boy, can this cause some real tensions. You have to give your friends and family time and your own patience as they adjust, while at the same time, let them know you are out of your box and the new you—the business owner, the healthier, thinner you— are here to stay! If they can't deal with this then we must move on. Life is short and going fast. They will have to catch up, or not.

As William Shakespeare said, "All the world's a stage and all the men (and women) are merely players." Just as clients and products come and go, people in your life have their purpose at different phases in your life. If it's not working for this phase, then find new people to surround yourself with the positive energy you will need for a healthy you… and a healthy, thriving business. When you are satisfied in your business life it directly affects the happiness at home.

Mentor Moment
As we say in the South, "If Mama ain't happy, ain't nobody happy."

Chapter 16
INTERVIEWS WITH ENTREPRENEURS

Interview with ROBERT HERNANDEZ
Owner: Seda France
Houston, TX
www.sedafrance.com

What is your philosophy as a business owner?
To create a great running company that gives me a lot of self satisfaction. I'm really hard to work with because I demand perfection. Nothing is fast enough for me. I don't like people who can't think or have no memory.

What prompted you to start your own business?
I was bored with what I was doing.

What excites you professionally?
I get excited about creating new products. Sourcing and traveling to find inspiration for the next new project.

What is your advice for a new company?
First thing is to get an operations and employee manual established. Get a good bookkeeper that you trust. Meet any and all friends in the same industry. Put everything in writing.

Do you have any personal advice?

A long time ago I read something that I loved: "Never hire anyone you wouldn't go to dinner with."

To what do you attribute your success?

My family, especially my father. He told me, "Don't let someone get ahead of you when you can do it yourself." Hiring the right people and surrounding myself with people that are smarter than me. My favorite saying is: "If you're going to do something, do it right!"

Interview with PAT BRADY
Owner: Label Tech, Inc.
Sommersworth, NH
www.labeltechinc.com

What is your philosophy as a business owner?

Produce quality merchandise at a reasonable profit and provide good customer service to keep them coming back.

What prompted you to start your own business?

Wow, that was twenty-three years ago. I had an entrepreneual spirit and wanted to be my own boss.

What excites you professionally?

Making a new deal for a new piece of business.

What is your advice for a new company?
Work hard and be prepared to make a lot of sacrifices. You may not get a paycheck for a while. You need to have a product or service that is viable for your market.

Do you have any personal advice?
Your personal life can become very intertwined with your business life, especially early on.

To what do you attribute your success?
Being in the right place at the right time for the market we were serving. We were able to produce the products that customers were demanding in a timely manner. I believe the key to our success was that we were always very customer oriented.

Interview with DON MEISNER, CFO

What is your philosophy as a CFO?
Balance both short and long term needs when making business decisions. Too often managers make decisions based solely on their desire to achieve short term results. Build strong relationships with customers, vendors and employees. A business needs to develop and maintain healthy relationships in order to be successful.

What excites you professionally?
I like the challenge of being able to come into a company and help set up the infrastructure. Working for a large company can stifle your individuality. A smaller business brings out the entrepreneurial spirit.

What is your advice for a new company?

Stay true to your core competency. Whatever got you to this point, stick with it.

Any personal advice?

Maintain a sense of humor. Enjoy life

INTERVIEW WITH LARRY BROWN
President: Clearly Fun Soap, Inc.
Griffin, GA
www.clearlyfunsoap.com

What is your philosophy as a president?

To build a business that can support and take care of my family and my employees' families. To create products that are fun and can make a difference to people. To establish a good work environment where you enjoy coming to work every day.

Why change careers and leave an established corporation?

The opportunity to join with a company in its early stages without the family element. It's a risk but can have great rewards. The challenge is fun.

What excites you about Clearly Fun Soap?

The challenge of growing a new business from the ground up. I enjoy seeing customers excited about our product.

What is your advice for a new company just getting started?

Hire people smarter than yourself. Make sure you are not under capitalized. Have a product you believe in and can grow through the markets.

Any personal advice?

Work hard. Establish a solid customer base. Stay focused. Keep your priorities straight. Make a To-Do-List every day and complete it. Always dress nice.

APPENDIX

CFS Mission Statement

We aim to make kids of all ages happy by providing the very best fun soap products available on the marketplace today. Our goal is to become the number one fun soap company in the United States by January 1, 2010.

Vision

To create the most unique fun soap products making folks happy and clean the world over.
"We aim to please"

Favorite websites

www.entrepreneur.com
www.inc.com
www.clearlyfunsoap.com

WHAT I ATE AND WHAT I DID TO LOSE THE WEIGHT AND KEEP IT OFF

I wish I had some magic pill or easy way out, but as far as I know there is none. However, our bodies are miraculous and with a little care they respond amazingly.

My diet was really a lifestyle change and went something like this: I tried to eat no more than 1500 calories a day. In the beginning I used a calorie counter book to get it exactly right. As time passed I was able to guess fairly accurately. I still do this even today. I keep a running tab in my head of the calories I've consumed. As I've said before I'm no expert so please consult a physician before doing anything drastic. I'm not a big breakfast eater but some mornings if I felt really hungry I would have a piece of multi-grain bread with a tiny bit of butter on it. I later would make 125-calorie bran muffins and put them in the freezer. I ate one every morning on the way to work. The recipe can be found in the resources section. For lunch I splurged almost every day with an "ice dream" from Chick-fil-A. A small one has approximately 250 calories. I only ate it at noontime, never at night. For 90% of my diet I ate salads. And more salads and more salads and when I thought I couldn't eat another one, I did. It was war and I, not my body, was going to win. It was my way of showing who was in control. I always had protein in my salad, whether it was chicken, beef or salmon. I also included a moderate amount of cheese and I used good dressings, none of that jelly low-fat stuff. I would control how much and not overdo the dressing, but I figured if I was eating a salad I wanted it to taste good. You still need to count your calories in your salad. You don't want to overdo it and have a 2400 calorie salad. Upon occasion I would vary and have lean meat with some vegetables for dinner, but mostly I ate salads. If you must have something sweet or fried don't beat yourself up over it just count it. If I had to have a bite of chocolate I would eat it early and only a small amount, but I always counted it. You will learn that you'd rather not because these things are high in calories and then you will find yourself still hungry. It's not easy losing weight. If it were, we would all be thin. It's WAR!! And you win by winning the daily battles. The best thing is the more battles you win the stronger you will become.

Now on to exercising. I had to lose 70 pounds before I even felt like exercising. I had not exercised in twenty years so I began with Curves. At first I was skeptical but I stuck with it. I went at least three times a week but mostly I went five times a week. After about eight weeks I began to see a change. I also walked at night. At first one mile, then two, then three, then four and finally five. I loved this the most. I would put my Ipod on and go. I think this is part of the success I had also. It was my favorite music and I would lose myself in it. As each song would begin I would say "oh, I love this song" and I'd keep going. I remember once when I was at Curves I had this feeling that my metabolism had fired back up after being dormant for decades. The weight began to come off even faster. Just when I should have been hitting that plateau my furnace kicked in and it seemed there was no stopping me. I had a goal to reach and I had to keep pace. My goal was to lose ten pounds a month and I did it no matter what. I watched the scale even though I hated that thing; but it was the measure of my success. After I had my tummy tuck to remove the excess skin I did not return to Curves but went to a local gym. I felt at this time that I needed to do more. I wake up and go to the gym before work. I don't like getting up and I try to talk myself out of it all the way there, but once I'm there, and especially when I'm finished, the feeling is unbelievable . Believe me, if I can do this you can too!!!!

After the weight was gone I panicked. How do I stop losing but more importantly how do I not gain it back? This was new uncharted territory for me. Again, it's not something I've conquered. It's a daily battle and learning experience. Sometimes if I let up in the least the weight will start to creep back on. I try to be aware of this and fix it fast. I am sure I will struggle with this the rest of my life and I've had to make peace with that. I have a lot at stake now and I have to keep this weight off. I've had a tummy tuck and I've written a book about loosing weight. Now that's pressure! It's all a very personal experience and each of you will do it differently—but never give up. Of all the things in this book, I hope this will help you the most. I know the struggles and the harsh reality of being overweight and I wish that on no one. I wish you the very best!

DAWN'S BRAN MUFFIN RECIPE

6 CUPS BRAN CEREAL

1 CUP APPLESAUCE

4 CUPS WHOLE WHEAT FLOUR

5 TSP. SODA

2 CUPS BOILING WATER

4 EGGS

1 ½ CUPS HONEY

½ CUP OATMEAL

½ CUP MILLER'S BRAN

½ CUP LIGHT BROWN SUGAR

1 CUP CHOPPED PECANS

2 PACKS DRIED CRANBERRIES

PREHEAT OVEN TO 400. COMBINE CEREAL AND BOILING WATER. STIR IN APPLESAUCE AND EGGS. ADD REMAINING INGREDIENTS. MIX. GREASE AND FLOUR PAN. BAKE 18-20 MINUTES.

Quote fromDawn's Daughter, Sarah (age 8 at time of writing)

I'm Sarah Carolyn Dallaire. My mom and dad own a soap business. I like stuff about it and I don't like stuff about it. What I like about Clearly Fun Soap is that we get a lot of money and cool soap. What I don't like is that my mom can't come home until 10:00 o'clock at night, but she gets to stay home in the day. My dad gets to come home, too.

I love my Mommy and Daddy!

U.S. SMALL BUSINESS ADMINISTRATION
WASHINGTON, D.C. 20416

FEB 2 5 2008

Ms. Dawn Dallaire
CEO
Clearly Fun Soap, Inc.
440 Wilson Road
Griffin, GA 30223

Dear Ms. Dallaire:

Congratulations! It is my pleasure to inform you that you have been selected as the 2008 Georgia Small Business Person of the Year.

Your hard work, innovative ideas, and dedication to your community have made you a success in your business. The U.S. Small Business Administration (SBA) is pleased to be able to recognize you for these achievements. As President Bush has said, "America's small businesses are the engine that drives our economy." You can be proud of the role you are playing in our Nation's robust economic growth.

Each year since 1963, the President has issued a proclamation calling for the celebration of Small Business Week. National Small Business Week recognizes outstanding small business owners for their personal successes and contributions to our Nation's economy. This year, SBA will honor the estimated 26.8 million small businesses in America. Small businesses represent more than 99 percent of all employers, provide 60 to 80 percent of the net new jobs, and generate a majority of American innovations.

As a State Small Business Person of the Year you are invited to represent Georgia and your business during National Small Business Week to be held in Washington, DC, April 21-23, 2008.

SBA has planned a series of events that should prove to be interesting, educational and enjoyable. You will soon receive additional information about National Small Business Week 2008.

Again, congratulations on your selection and I look forward to meeting you in April.

Sincerely yours,

Steve Preston

Federal Recycling Program   Printed on Recycled Paper

121

clearly fun soap™